COMPREHENSIVE RESEARCH
AND STUDY GUIDE

Dante

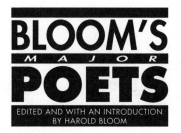

BLOOM'S MAJOR POETS

EDITED AND WITH AN INTRODUCTION
BY HAROLD BLOOM

BLOOM'S MAJOR SHORT STORY WRITERS

Anton Chekhov

Joseph Conrad

Stephen Crane

William Faulkner

F. Scott Fitzgerald

Nathaniel Hawthorne

Ernest Hemingway

O. Henry

Shirley Jackson

Henry James

James Joyce

D. H. Lawrence

Jack London

Herman Melville

Flannery O'Connor

Edgar Allan Poe

Katherine Anne Porter

J. D. Salinger

John Steinbeck

Mark Twain

John Updike

Eudora Welty

BLOOM'S MAJOR WORLD POETS

Maya Angelou

Robert Browning

Geoffrey Chaucer

Samuel T. Coleridge

Dante

Emily Dickinson

John Donne

T. S. Eliot

Robert Frost

Homer

Langston Hughes

John Keats

John Milton

Sylvia Plath

Edgar Allan Poe

Poets of World War I

Shakespeare's Poems & Sonnets

Percy Shelley

Alfred, Lord Tennyson

Walt Whitman

William Wordsworth

William Butler Yeats

COMPREHENSIVE RESEARCH
AND STUDY GUIDE

Dante

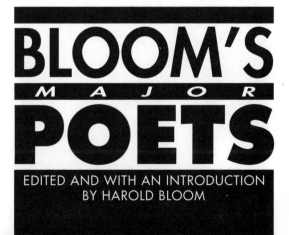

BLOOM'S *MAJOR* POETS

EDITED AND WITH AN INTRODUCTION
BY HAROLD BLOOM

© 2001 by Chelsea House Publishers, a subsidiary of
Haights Cross Communications.

Introduction © 2001 by Harold Bloom.

Printed and bound in the United States of America.

First Printing
1 3 5 7 9 8 6 4 2

Library of Congress Cataloging-in-Publication Data

Dante / edited with an introduction by Harold Bloom
    p. cm.—(Bloom's major poets)
    Includes bibliographical references and index.
    ISBN 0-7910-5939-1 (alk. paper)
    1. Dante Alighieri, 1265–1321—Criticism and interpretation.
    I. Bloom, Harold. II. Series.

  PQ4390.D27 2000
  851'.1--dc21   00-064452
                                CIP

Chelsea House Publishers
1974 Sproul Road, Suite 400
Broomall, PA 19008-0914

The Chelsea House World Wide Web address is
http://www.chelseahouse.com

Contributing Editor: Emmy Chang

Produced by: Robert Gerson Publisher's Services, Santa Barbara, CA

Contents

User's Guide

This volume is designed to present biographical, critical, and bibliographical information on the author's best-known or most important poems. Following Harold Bloom's editor's note and introduction is a detailed biography of the author, discussing major life events and important literary accomplishments. A thematic and structural analysis of each poem follows, tracing significant themes, patterns, and motifs in the work.

A selection of critical extracts, derived from previously published material from leading critics, analyzes aspects of each poem. The extracts consist of statements from the author, if available, early reviews of the work, and later evaluations up to the present. A bibliography of the author's writings (including a complete list of all books written, cowritten, edited, and translated), a list of additional books and articles on the author and the work, and an index of themes and ideas in the author's writings conclude the volume.

~

Harold Bloom is Sterling Professor of the Humanities at Yale University and Henry W. and Albert A. Berg Professor of English at the New York University Graduate School. He is the author of over 20 books, including *Shelley's Mythmaking* (1959), *The Visionary Company* (1961), *Blake's Apocalypse* (1963), *Yeats* (1970), *A Map of Misreading* (1975), *Kabbalah and Criticism* (1975), *Agon: Toward a Theory of Revisionism* (1982), *The American Religion* (1992), *The Western Canon* (1994), and *Omens of Millennium: The Gnosis of Angels, Dreams, and Resurrection* (1996). *The Anxiety of Influence* (1973) sets forth Professor Bloom's provocative theory of the literary relationships between the great writers and their predecessors. His most recent books include *Shakespeare: The Invention of the Human,* a 1998 National Book Award finalist, and *How to Read and Why,* which was published in 2000.

Professor Bloom earned his Ph.D. from Yale University in 1955 and has served on the Yale faculty since then. He is a 1985 MacArthur Foundation Award recipient, served as the Charles Eliot Norton Professor of Poetry at Harvard University in 1987–88, and has received honorary degrees from the universities of Rome and Bologna. In 1999, Professor Bloom received the prestigious American Academy of Arts and Letters Gold Medal for Criticism.

Currently, Harold Bloom is the editor of numerous Chelsea House volumes of literary criticism, including the series BLOOM'S NOTES, BLOOM'S MAJOR DRAMATISTS, BLOOM'S MAJOR NOVELISTS, MAJOR LITERARY CHARACTERS, MODERN CRITICAL VIEWS, MODERN CRITICAL INTERPRETATIONS, and WOMEN WRITERS OF ENGLISH AND THEIR WORKS.

Editor's Note

My Introduction essentially contrasts Dante with Shakespeare, since they are the two most eminent Western poets.

As some thirty-one distinguished Critical Views are excerpted in this volume, I must confine myself to mentioning those that mean most to my own experience of reading Dante.

The *Vita Nuova* is crucially contextualized by Charles S. Singleton, while Giuseppe Mazzotta clarifies the relation of Dante's poetic language to the difficulties of representing transcendence.

Dante's *Stony Rhymes,* including the magnificent sestina, "To the Dim Light and the large Circle of Shade," receive informative commentaries from Margaret Spanos, and the joint effort of Ronald L. Martinez and Robert M. Durling.

The great English Romantic critic William Hazlitt powerfully emphasizes Dante's originality, while major insights into the *Inferno* are provided by Francesco de Sanctis on Ugolino, Kenneth Gross on the relation of crimes to punishments, and Teodolinda Barolini on Ulysses.

I find Karl Vossler and Peter Dronke particularly illuminating on the *Purgatorio,* after which A. C. Charity, John Freccero, and Robin Kirkpatrick make essential observations upon *Paradiso.*

Introduction

As Homer and the Hebrew Bible share the ultimate aesthetic eminence of the West in the ancient world, even so Dante and Shakespeare divide up the Sublime in what remains the Western culture of the last seven centuries. James Joyce and T. S. Eliot both would like to have preferred Dante to Shakespeare, but each realized that: "I would have to take the Englishman, because he is richer," as Joyce wryly phrased it. To the poets, Dante has been "the Book and School of the Ages" (Stefan George's formulation). The reader, ideally, is alone with the *Commedia*, whereas Shakespeare's stage mediates his figures for us. We hardly can know who Shakespeare was; even in the Sonnets he seems estranged from himself. Despite Dante's extraordinary personages—Farinata, Manfred, Brunetto Latini; Ulysses, Ugolino, Francesca and so many more, Virgil and Beatrice foremost among them—his greatest figure is Dante the Pilgrim, by no means identical with Dante the poet. If you can imagine Hamlet transmuted into a Pilgrim of Eternity, commenting upon the realities of Hell, Purgatory, and Heaven, then you can begin to apprehend the unique power of Dante the Pilgrim.

Dante regarded himself as an authentic prophet, and gives us his *Commedia*, in effect, as the Third Testament, at least as much an authority as the Hebrew Bible and the Greek New Testament. Shakespeare avoided revelations or the solving of spiritual problems, other than very indirectly. We have learned that Shakespeare gives us truth, as Chaucer and Cervantes do, but Dante (like Milton and Blake after him) insists that he enlightens us with *the* truth itself. Dante's extraordinary bitterness, like his astonishing exaltation, is justified by the solitary grandeur of his quest. You do not quarrel with Dante, any more than you would with the first Isaiah, the prophet. The spiritual audacity of Dante is absolute: he is Isaiah and Joachim of Flora fused together. You can resist Dante, but only in the name of a poet-prophet roughly equal to him, a John Milton or William Blake. Yet your resistance will be overcome cognitively and aesthetically, even if you hold out spiritually against Dante's immense drive and comprehensiveness of vision.

Dante, as the Twenty-First century begins, can seem the most difficult of all poets. By this, I do not mean just that he is a learned poet, deeply grounded in St. Augustine and the Scholastics. American Dante criticism—particularly of the school of Erich

Auerbach, Charles Singleton, and John Freccero—is rather too likely to give the impression that Dante versifies Christian doctrine. Italian critics, Benedetto Croce among them, have warned us that poetry dominates in Dante. Ernest Robert Curtius, the strongest of modern German scholarly critics, argued that Dante's vision is a private *gnosis* that cannot fully be expounded. Though he lived to finish the *Commedia*, Dante hoped to achieve a personal synthesis that he associated with reaching the mystically "perfect" age of eighty-one. Though the Church has been happy to subsume Dante, no reader should forget that Beatrice is the poet's own creation, and no part of the Church's hierarchy. There are mysterious elements in the *Commedia* that remain signs of Dante's originality and creative audacity. Who has been subsumed, the Church or Dante?

There is a tradition of reading, in which one prefers the *Inferno* in one's youth, the *Purgatorio* in the middle years, and the *Paradiso* in old age. Approaching seventy, I still concentrate on the *Purgatorio*, which has influenced modern poetry much more extensively than the *Paradiso* has done. And yet only Dante, of all Western poets, has been able to write Paradise. Shakespeare, whose quest was to secularize transcendence, turns back in his final work—his portion of *The Two Noble Kinsmen*—to "that which is" in order to "leave dispute / That are above our question." That remains the singular audacity in which Dante might seem to be beyond Shakespeare. Yet I hardly know what "beyond Shakespeare" can mean. Dante's Ulysses speaks out of the infernal fire, and affirms a quest beyond limits. We do not know why Dante faints in response, though we can surmise that Ulysses may speak for something in Dante that also is beyond all limits. Perhaps no one, anywhere in the plays, speaks for something in Shakespeare himself, though I tend to think otherwise, especially in regard to Hamlet and Falstaff. Shakespeare was not a Pilgrim. Dante, Pilgrim and Poet-Prophet, is in one sense the anti-Shakespeare, your alternative if your own spirit will not accept Shakespeare's wisdom in choosing "that which is." ❀

Biography of
Dante Alighieri

Dante Alighieri was born in Florence in May or June of 1265. (The exact date of his birth is unknown, but in the *Paradiso*, he stated that he was born when the sun was in Gemini, indicating that his birthday was sometime between the 18th of May and the 17th of June.) His baptismal name was Durante, but the name was later contracted into Dante, and he was the son of Alighiero di Bellincione d'Alighiero, a moneylender, and his first wife Bella. Though descended of noble stock—some accounts trace the Alighieris' lineage to the founders of Rome—the family had fallen on harder times, and by Dante's day they belonged to the city's artisan class.

Dante's family were of modest means, but he was given a solid training in classical and medieval Latin; he had access as well to the contemporary literature of France. Self-taught as a writer of verse, he met Guido Cavalcanti through the exchange and discussion of love poetry, and he may possibly have studied under Brunetto Latini. Dante's marriage to Gemma Donati, arranged by his father in 1277, is believed to have taken place in 1285. The union would produce four children, three sons and a daughter.

Most of our knowledge of Dante's early life is culled from the account he himself gives in the *Vita Nuova* (The New Life), an amalgam of poetry and prose detailing his initial encounters with the lady Beatrice. He first saw Beatrice Portinari, his lifelong love, when they were both nine, in 1274. Historically, nothing indicates that she ever returned his passion, and Dante did not meet her again until he was 18. She was married at an early age to another man, but neither this nor Dante's own marriage interfered with his platonic devotion to her. He enshrined Beatrice in the *Vita Nuova* as his vision of grace, and she would remain for him a lifelong source of moral and literary inspiration. Although Beatrice was never an active part of Dante's life in any way, her influence over him and his family must have been immense. Years later, after her father's death, his daughter became a nun and took the name of Sister Beatrice.

In 1289 Dante fought in the cavalry for Florence. The following year, in 1290, Beatrice died. With her death, Dante's feelings for her only intensified. As a way to deal with his grief, he became engrossed in the study of the classics, religion, and philosophy, particularly the works of Boethius and Cicero. The Lady Philosophy, the poet claimed in his unfinished *Convivio* (The Banquet), made him "so keenly aware of her sweetness that the love of her drove away and destroyed every other thought." The Dante of this period believed philosophy or rhetoric alone could lead to ultimate truth—a belief he eventually recanted, much as Beatrice (Grace) supplanted Virgil (Reason) in the course of the pilgrim's progress through the *Commedia*.

Dante was never merely a philosopher isolated from real life; while he followed intellectual pursuits, he also concerned himself actively with the fates of his city and of the Christian world. From his early days soldiering to his participation in various councils of state (including the Consiglio dei Cento, or Council of the Hundred), he showed a fierce devotion to Florence. In 1295 he joined the Guild of Physicians and Apothecaries, and from there he moved to public office. In 1300 he served as one of Florence's seven priors. Political involvement eventually influenced both his literary work and his personal fortunes, when civil war ravaged the city.

The Guelph party that ruled Florence split into two factions, known as "Whites" and "Blacks." Dante supported the Whites, but in 1301, while he was on an embassy mission to the Pope in Rome, the tide turned against Dante's faction. Dante was sentenced to death should he return to Florence. Stranded in Rome, Dante found himself an exile.

Dante probably never saw his home again. The humiliation of depending on others for his livelihood was apparently not easy; he wrote that he had learned "how salt is the taste of another man's bread and how hard is the way up and down another man's stairs." During this difficult time, Dante's creativity flourished, however. In 1307 he began the epic poem *Divinia Commedia* (Divine Comedy), his spiritual testament made up of the *Inferno*, the *Purgatorio*, and the *Paradiso*.

Although exiled from his city, Dante continued to be politically active. He was vehemently opposed to the theocratic papacy of Boniface, and he composed a number of letters supporting the crowning of Henry VII as emperor. With Henry's death in 1313, however, Dante's hopes for "two suns" of governance—for church *and* state, rather than church alone—were permanently ended. His

De monarchia was formally condemned, and Dante himself only narrowly escaped excommunication.

Through his last two decades he traveled from city to city, living under the protection of assorted nobles. In 1317 he settled in Ravenna, and he lived there for the rest of his life. Although he never saw his wife again, his children and some of his grandchildren may have accompanied him during his last years in Ravenna.

In the midst of his trials, Dante finished the *Commedia*. Slandered, an outcast, living by the kindness of strangers, Dante came to view his hundred cantos of *terza rima* as far more than an artistic endeavor: they were a labor of love, conceived to redeem his name and, ultimately, to save his city. In their way, too, they were an act of contrition. In the *Purgatorio*, one section of the *Commedia*, Dante personally reveals himself in the penances of pride, wrath, and lust. Perhaps these were the areas where he felt he had sinned most in life. The poem closes, however, with all powers of knowing and loving fulfilled and consumed by the understanding's union with the Divine Essence, "the Love that moves the sun and other stars."

Dante completed the *Commedia*, which he dedicated to Can Grande della Scala, only a few years before his death. His other late writings include the Latin *Eclogues* and the *Quaestio de aqua et terra* (Discourse on the Nature of Water and Earth), a lecture on land and water masses.

Dante died of malaria in September 1321. He was a great political thinker and philosopher, as well as a poet. Today he is considered to be one of the world's greatest writers. ❀

Thematic Analysis of the
Vita Nuova

The *Vita Nuova*, Dante's earliest published work, investigates the awakenings brought on by the experience of love. It comprises two concurrent narratives: a series of love poems and a prose commentary on both the poems and the events giving rise to them. Dante stresses the selectiveness of the compilation, telling us he wrote "divers rhymes ⟨. . .⟩ whereof I shall here write only as much as concerneth the most gentle Beatrice, which is but a very little." It should thus be kept constantly in mind that, even taken as literally as the text allows, the *Vita Nuova* cannot be regarded as a memoir. Rather, it is a kind of palimpsest, glossing older events into a newer commentary on the poet's "new life."

The events of the *Vita Nuova* are easily told. The young Dante, aged nine, meets a girl "who was called Beatrice by many who knew not wherefore" (**Canto II**). Debate has raged for centuries over whether Dante's Beatrice does or does not correspond to Folco Portinari's daughter Bice; if she does, Dante here presumably intends to say that her name meant "she who gives blessing," and those who called her "Beatrice" did so without realizing she was indeed a giver of blessings.

The girl is dressed in red. Dante, looking upon her, feels the spirit of love stirring in him until it becomes overpowering. Nine years later (**Canto III**) he sees her again, this time in white. She greets him, "with so virtuous a bearing that I seemed then and there to behold the very limits of blessedness." He has in sleep a vision of Love (*Amore*), who bears Beatrice in his arms and feeds her Dante's flaming heart before ascending heavenward. Waking, Dante composes a poem narrating the incident.

Watching Beatrice in church one day (**Canto V**), he is thought to be staring at another lady, and he decides to encourage the deception to conceal his real love—a standard ploy of courtly romance. Away from home, the poet is again visited by Love and instructed to adopt a new screen lady (**Canto IX**), but on doing so he finds Beatrice will no longer greet him (**Canto X**). Love explains her reaction and instructs him to compose a new poem (**Canto XII**). (Dante's figure of Love is an odd one, offering contradictory advice and speaking sometimes in Italian, sometimes in Latin.)

Dante next encounters Beatrice at a wedding party, where he is overcome by her presence even before seeing her. Mocked by the guests, he returns home and weeps (**Canto XIV**), and asks himself why he should continue to love the lady when the experience affords him nothing (**Canto XV**). When asked of his love, Dante tells a woman that as Beatrice will no longer grant him her salutation, he now can find blessing only in praising her. The woman points out that he has not been doing this (**Canto XVIII**). Taken aback, he resolves henceforth to write only in praise of his lady and composes the best known of the *Vita Nuova's* poems, *Donne che avete intelletto d'Amore* ("Ladies that have intelligence in Love") (**Canto XIX**).

Soon afterward, Beatrice's father dies (**Canto XXI**). Illness and sorrow make Dante realize that Beatrice, too, will one day die, and in delirium he dreams of her death (**Canto XXIII**).

Dante sees Giovanna, his friend Cavalcanti's beloved, who is made to precede Beatrice as John (from whose name "Giovanna" is derived) preceded Christ (**Canto XXIV**). There follows a digression in which Dante disavows the figure of Love as a mere trope (**Canto XXV**). After this come more poems, one of which is broken off (**Canto XXVII**) at the news of Beatrice's death.

Dante is asked by a friend to write in praise of a lady who has recently died, and ultimately composes two poems (**cantos XXXIII–XXXIV**). (Scholars believe the friend may have been Beatrice's brother Manetto.) On the anniversary of Beatrice's death, Dante is sketching an angel when he becomes aware of people around him, whom he greets and to whom he addresses a sonnet (**Canto XXXV**). In his sadness he begins to fall in love with a lady who looks on him pityingly from a window (the *donna pietosa*), and in poetry wonders if he might rediscover love in her (**Canto XXXVI**). He then deplores his own fickleness (**Canto XXXVIII**), composing a dialogue between Heart (appetite) and Soul (reason) (**Canto XXXIX**). A vision of Beatrice appears as he first saw her, and he vows in a sonnet to return to his love (**Canto XL**). There follow two more poems (**cantos XLI–XLII**), and a final resolve to say nothing more of Beatrice until he may one day write of her "what hath not before been written of any woman" (**Canto XLIII**)—a line widely read as a foreshadowing of the *Commedia*.

The *Vita Nuova* follows the forms and conventions of a 13th century school of poetry that Dante called *dolce stil novo*—the "sweet new style." Stilnovist poets used eulogistic terms: Dante constantly associates his lady with humility, with charity, and with all virtue, in poetry that seems elegiac even before her death. The important question for all Stilnovist poets was: What is love? Answers varied. **Canto XIX** of the *Vita Nuova, Donne che avete intelletto d'Amore,* was hailed as a high-water mark of stilnovist poetry. But Dante was no mere exponent of an existing theory of love. Above all else, his *Vita Nuova* shattered the courtly paradigm by allowing for the beloved's death.

From the outset, the Provençal ideals which gave rise to stilnovism inevitably collided with Christian belief. A blatant example of the clash may be found in Giacomo da Lentini's "Io m'aggio posto," whose speaker resolves in line 1 to serve God and reach paradise— then admits in line 4, *Sanza mia donna non vi voria gire.* ("Without my lady I do not wish to go.") The conflict seemed irreconcilable, for either God or the lady had to hold first place in the soul. As a result, one could not be both a Christian and a troubadour, and in fact most troubadours solved the problem by simply prudently recanting in time for the afterlife. What Dante provided, or began to provide, was a synthesis of the Christian and chivalric codes. His innovation was to posit that the love of a lady, far from disrupting the Christian faith, could in fact lead to the love of God. The *Vita Nuova's* assertion that "Whoso deserves not Heaven / May never hope to have her company" would seem a forthright answer to da Lentini's dilemma: for Dante, there was simply no question of a paradise without Beatrice. His lady was herself "the beatitude which is the goal of desire."

Multiple meanings permeate the *Vita Nuova,* often embedded in the language itself. The ambiguities begin as early as the title, for *nuova* bears a connotation not only of "new" but also of "wonderful" or "strange." Likewise, when Dante alludes to his "gracious lady," the phrase could refer to a purely secular or a wholly divine kind of grace, and more frequently refers to both. Equally faceted readings are invited by Beatrice's "salutation," for *salute* means not only "greeting" but also "salvation," and Christ himself is *salus nostra,* our salvation.

Who is Beatrice? Dante's language, in describing Love, echoes the Angel revealing the Resurrection in the Gospel of Mark. Ultimately, the vision of Beatrice's death inescapably recalls the Crucifixion, with the sun going out, stars weeping, birds falling. Scholars have speculated on the "representative" meaning of everything from the color of Beatrice's dress (representing the blood of Christ?) to the identity of the *donna pietosa* (possibly the Lady Philosophy?)—but such readings too easily stray from the text. A safer approach is to regard the work as analogical, leaving a clear distance between its literal and divine interpretations; thus Beatrice may be as Christ without necessarily *being* Christ. Also, the Beatrice of the *Vita Nuova* is not, or not yet, the Beatrice of the *Commedia*.

Dante Gabriel Rossetti had so little patience with Dante's commentaries on these poems that he left them to his brother to translate. As the origin of a new theory of love, however—and as the germ of Beatrice's apotheosis—the *Vita Nuova* disintegrates without its prose. Countless young men idolized their ladies, and nearly as many wrote poems to them. But whether its progress is one of spiritual or of literary conversion, what makes the *Vita Nuova* unique is that retrospective "gloss" made upon a very young poet by the same poet, slightly older, as he schooled himself gradually to become the Dante the world remembers. ❀

Critical Views on
the *Vita Nuova*

CHARLES S. SINGLETON ON DANTE'S BOOK OF MEMORY

[Charles S. Singleton (1909–1985) was a professor of Romance Languages at the Johns Hopkins University. He was the author of *Commedia* (1954) and *Journey to Beatrice* (1958), and of translations of the *Book of the Courtier* (1959) and the *Divine Comedy* (1970). His *Essay* (1949) proposes a strongly allegorical reading of the *Vita Nuova*, especially of the prose. In this extract, Singleton considers Dante's poem and examines its implications for the rest of the work.]

Even the most attentive reader of the *Vita Nuova* may have been unaware up to this point that the book had any such thing as a proem. As such, it will not be indicated in any edition that he may have of the work. However, "the proem which precedes this little book" ⟨chapter XXVIII⟩ cannot be other than what in all editions is printed as the first chapter of the work, a chapter only two sentences long. ⟨. . .⟩

In that part of the book of my memory before which little could be read is found a rubric which says: INCIPIT VITA NOVA [Here beginneth the New Life]. Under which rubric I find written the words which it is my intention to copy into this little book; and if not all, at least their substance. ⟨. . .⟩

⟨B⟩y this image the whole work is cast into a mold which constitutes the first outline of its form. ⟨. . .⟩ And since, as far along as chapter XXVIII and the actual death of Beatrice, the reader is still referred back to this figure of a book at the beginning, it is important that we see from the outset what its implications are. ⟨. . .⟩

Briefly, the situation is this: some parts of this Book of Memory were written in the past and some are being written now. The poems belong to the past. And that prose which stands around the poems in the original Book of Memory also belongs to the past. But let us remember that not all of the prose in the copy we have was found in the original. For here and there the scribe has added to that original text, and his additions are glosses. They are conceived in the present tense.

Of course, we know that the *prose* which the poet finds already inscribed in the original, and which is therefore in the past tense, is not his. For that prose actually is prose only through metaphor. The "words" which compose it are words only by virtue of a figure which gives them such metaphorical meaning. They are in reality not words at all but real things and events. ⟨. . .⟩

We remember now that the Proem has said that these words were *found* in the Book of his Memory. ⟨. . .⟩

⟨T⟩o the reader of that century, already and without any metaphor of a "book of memory," it was possible, even reasonable, to regard the things and events of our real world as so many words in a book, the Book of the Created Universe. ⟨. . .⟩

Now the work of poets ought to resemble the work of God, ought, like His creation, to be addressed to a reasonable reader and be susceptible of the same exegetical methods. ⟨. . .⟩

⟨T⟩hese pages of a Book of Memory, already filled with a prose not written by human hand, give foundation to the presence of mysteries; and this scribe making his copy, and poring over the pages, and finding new meaning in them, makes the revelation itself of those mysteries possible by providing for an eye that can see them and a time when they may be seen.

—Charles S. Singleton, *An Essay on the Vita Nuova* (Baltimore: Johns Hopkins University Press, 1949): pp. 26, 27, 34–35, 37, 48, 54.

BERNARD S. LEVY ON THE GOSPEL OF JOHN AND *VITA NUOVA* XLI

[Bernard S. Levy is Professor Emeritus of English at the State University of New York, Binghamton. He has edited *Developments in the Early Renaissance* (1972), *The Alliterative Tradition in the Fourteenth Century* (1981), and *The Bible in the Middle Ages: Its Influence on Literature and*

Art (1992). Here, Levy suggests that the "sigh" prompted by Beatrice's smile [XXVI] deliberately parallels Christ's breath of the Holy Spirit (John 20:19–31), elevating a human, courtly love into an experience of divine reverence and grace.]

⟨T⟩he poetry is even stronger than the prose ⟨in XXVI⟩ in its evocations. In his description of Beatrice's greeting, he characterizes his lady in such a way as to suggest Christ. ⟨. . .⟩ He then suggests that from Beatrice's lips moves a sweet spirit so full of love that it penetrates to the soul and tells it to sigh: ⟨XXVI, 7⟩.

At first sight, the image seems to be merely the action of the courtly lady upon the lover in inspiring him with love; in such a case, the inspiration moves from the heart of the beloved and through her eyes, then enters the eyes of the lover and penetrates to his heart, prompting the sigh that is expected of such a lover in the presence of his lady. But the evocations of Christ and the particular action described indicate that Dante is concerned in this sonnet with a much higher spiritual love than has been suggested previously, especially in the description of the inspiration of the lady as the spirit of love moves from her lips to the soul of the beholder. The concatenation of images suggests that Dante had in mind as analogue the scene following Christ's Resurrection in which Christ breathes the Holy Spirit—the Spirit of Love—upon his disciples. The scene occurs within a passage from the Gospel of John ⟨20:19-31⟩ which includes reference both to Thomas the Apostle's initial doubts and subsequent belief at the sight of the resurrected Christ and to the idea that what is written in the Gospel is recorded for those who have not seen. ⟨. . .⟩

The sighs inspired by Beatrice in fact totally change after her death. At first they express despondency and a wish for death, as in the sonnet *Venite a intender li sospiri miei* (XXXII, 5–6) and in the second stanza of the canzone *Quantunque volte . . .* (XXXIII, 7–8), respectively. Later in the vision of Beatrice in glory (XXXIX), Dante's sighs inspired by the memory of Beatrice are accompanied by tears of repentance for his forgetting of Beatrice and for his infatuation with the Lady of the Window. These intermediary steps prepare for the final sonnet, *Oltre la spera*, in which the sigh rising from Dante's heart is transformed into a pilgrim spirit, and, drawn on high by a new understanding of love achieved through the tears, ascends to heaven to experience something analogous to the Beatific Vision in its view of Beatrice in glory. ⟨. . .⟩

It is in fact this final image that initiates Dante's new life in love, in the spiritual sense, for it is his entire experience of his beloved Beatrice in the *Vita Nuova*, moving gradually from a physical to a spiritual love, that forms the basis for Dante's new life both spiritually and poetically. Thus, in the final chapter and the final words of the *libello*, he prays that his soul—like his sigh—may ascend to behold the glory of its lady, the blessed Beatrice ⟨XLII, 3⟩. ⟨. . .⟩

The question proposed earlier—How is Dante, in the final sonnet of the *Vita Nuova*, able to send a sigh from his heart to heaven which can behold his lady Beatrice in glory?—can now be answered. It is only by making Beatrice analogous to Christ and through the specific allusion to the account in the Gospel of John of Christ's breathing the Holy Spirit into the souls of men that Dante's sigh is transformed from the involuntary exhalation of the young lover into a spiritual entity which can transcend earthly limitations and achieve a foretaste of the heavenly vision more fully described by the poet in the *Commedia*.

—Bernard S. Levy, "Beatrice's Greeting and Dante's 'Sigh' in the *Vita Nuova*," *Dante Studies with the Annual Report of the Dante Society* 92 (August 1974): pp. 58–59, 60–62.

JAMES T. S. WHEELOCK ON THE SYNTHESIS OF CHRISTIAN AND COURTLY LOVES

[James T. S. Wheelock has taught at the University of Colorado. In this extract, he suggests that Dante uses the figure of Love to resolve the disjunction between the ideals of troubadour romance and Christian *caritas*.]

⟨G⟩iven the objective of portraying a Beatrice that participated in a "dual" nature of *Salvatrix dantis* and erotic object, he had the consequent task of reconciling two traditions that were in their purest, unaccommodated states, structurally incompatible. ⟨. . .⟩

The connotative values of the two figures—the totalitarian, aloof *midons* on the one hand and the egalitarian, self-effacing Christ on the other—were ⟨...⟩ diametrically opposed. ⟨...⟩

⟨P⟩otential incoherence was avoided by investing the persona of Amore with that portion of the attributes of the familiar *midons* which would have fit uncomfortably on the Beatrice "benignamente d'umiltà vestuta." ⟨...⟩

If the quasi-miraculous *virtù* of her comportment is characterized by the *aurea mediocritas* of "misura" (XIX, 11), this same "benign humility" (XXIV, 6) is confirmed by the spatial context in which we find Beatrice consistently depicted. ⟨...⟩ In each instance of their meeting, Beatrice is described as being not in an exalted position vis-à-vis the poet, but on the same physical plane. The schema is unvaried and receives the full weight of the narrator's insistence. ⟨...⟩

⟨A⟩ particularly illustrative moment occurs when Beatrice denies Dante his *guerdon*, but not as we might expect with the slightest hint of *alterigia*. On the contrary her act is a non-act ("mi negò") and is accomplished (and the phrase's syntactical positioning gives stress to the thought) as she passed alongside the poet ("passando per alcuna parte" [X, 2]).

Quite unlike the love objects of her "courtly" antecedents, Beatrice in the *Vita nuova* without exception is described in the later events occurring in her lifetime as moving among other *donne gentili* that are her peers and along a route that in no way removes her from their social or physical context. ⟨...⟩

Dante's problem ⟨...⟩ was dramatic as well as philosophical. Absolute *mediocritas*, as elegant and nearly miraculous as it may be, and beatification, even when physically exhilarating, do not constitute the stuff of which erotic lyricism is made. ⟨...⟩

⟨T⟩he presence by a kind of division of labor of the dominating Amore figure made it possible for Dante to draw upon the generous repertoire of empassioned terminology common to the Provençal, Sicilian and *stilnovista* literary schools without reducing his uniquely benevolent lady to the form of the traditional *domna*. ⟨...⟩ As his "altissimo sire" (VI, 2), Amore lords it over Dante with absolute control throughout the first half of the *Vita nuova*. His domination is consistent up until the moment when, during the transition we have observed at the end of XVIII and the opening of XIX, there is a shifting of *propositi* and the poet turns his attention exclusively to "quelle parole che lodano la donna mia" (XVIII, 8). After this juncture, according to the definition of her "stato gentile" specified in the *canzone* of XIX, any mention of the detrimental effects of love on Dante's psyche would have been extraneous to his purpose (as were the particulars of Beatrice's death). ⟨. . .⟩

One final confirmation of the notion that Amore exists in the *Vita nuova* primarily to perform this function of domination is in the realization that there is no need for him to reappear in association with Dante's encounter with the "donna de la finestra." The nature of her role combines in a more traditional manner the qualities of tyrannical dominance and gratuitous consolation the poet calls "pietà."

—James T. S. Wheelock, "A Function of the *Amore* Figure in the *Vita Nuova*," *Romanic Review* 68, no. 4 (November 1977): pp. 277, 278, 279, 280, 281–82, 283, 284–85.

GIUSEPPE MAZZOTTA ON IMAGINATION AND TRANSCENDENCE

[Giuseppe Mazzotta is a professor of Italian at Yale University. He is the author of *Dante, Poet of the Desert: History and Allegory in the* Divine Comedy (1979), *The World at Play in Boccaccio's* Decameron (1986), and *Dante's Vision and the Circle of Knowledge* (1993). Here, Mazzotta reads the *Vita Nuova* as an "apprenticeship" that moves away from the contingencies of memory and time. Only by freeing himself from a view of imagination as passive—as reactive rather than active—can the fledgling poet of *dolce stil novo* become the author of the visionary *Commedia*.]

⟨T⟩he *Vita Nuova* ⟨is⟩ a parable of a poetic apprenticeship. ⟨. . .⟩

The pattern I have summarily delineated re-focuses on the issue that is central to ⟨it⟩. The lover is bound to a world of pure images and representations. The pilgrims go to Rome to see Christ's image; the lover draws the picture of an angel or is absorbed in the images of his memory. But the section also dramatizes the lover's predicament: in a world of images the fabric of stable references seems to be on the verge of dissolving and no necessary bond seems to exist between images and their referents. The lover discovers that the destination of his texts can be arranged and simulated. Early in the narrative (chapter V) the lady of the screen was a strategy of deception to protect the purity of the poet's love for Beatrice, but there too, the simulation acquired a reality that creates a crisis between Beatrice and the lover. Now Dante has to warn us that on careful examination of the two stanzas of the *canzone* he writes for his friend one can clearly see that "diverse persone parlano." More cogently, Dante now discovers that the persistence of memory is endangered by forgetfulness, that his love can be replaced, and that for all her uniqueness, the image of Beatrice can be doubled by the "donna gentile."

The awareness of the constitutive ambiguities of the language of representation ushers in the imaginative leap of the final paragraph of the *Vita Nuova*; at this point the *Vita Nuova* more than a selection of reminiscences from the past is the adumbration of the book to come, the book of the future—"spero di dicer di lei quello che mai non fue detto d'alcuna." We are not given a description of the "mirabile visione." We are simply told that the mind cannot grasp it nor words yet tell of it. This is the journey of the poetic imagination, the conviction of poetry's absolute privilege to be the profound means of exploring the world of the dead and bring them back to life. The *Vita Nuova* begins by resuscitating the images of memory, as if memory were the path to essences, and ends with a visionary venture into the future. The future, earlier, was at one with death; now it is the project to write. To the interpretability of memory, Dante substitutes the enigma of the future. In the openness of the *Vita Nuova*'s end, he also gives up the thought of the poet who passively waits for inspiration, and promises, on the contrary, to strive and study in order to write. The imagination is unveiled not just as a power to give a replica of one's thoughts and impressions. It is the activity that "places" the poet between images and their referents, in the heart of the split between the two, from where the poet can seek unknown worlds and prepare for the future possible encounter with Beatrice across the barrier of death.

—Giuseppe Mazzotta, "The Language of Poetry in the *Vita Nuova*," *Rivista di Studi Italiani* 1, no. 1 (April 1983): pp. 3, 12–13.

[Robert Pogue Harrison is an associate professor of French
and Italian at Stanford University. His books include *The
Murano Workshop* (1979), *The Body of Beatrice* (1988), and
Forests: The Shadow of Civilization (1992). In this extract,
Harrison examines Dante's philosophic differences with
another poet of the "sweet new style," Guido Cavalcanti
("the first among my friends" [III]), to whom the *Vita
Nuova* is dedicated and who will later be given a cameo in
Inferno X.]

Dante does not suspect that Beatrice is among the women gathered
⟨in XIV⟩ and, standing in the room unawares, he feels a tremor in the
left side of his body. ⟨. . .⟩

The scene epitomizes what I have tried to stress about Beatrice:
that her *presence* and her *appearance* must be thought of as a unity,
yet differentiated. Before Beatrice is perceived with the eyes, her
presence already induces physiological disorder in her lover. As the
locus of presence, her body precedes and at the same time withdraws
behind her phenomenality, such that presence and appearance form
a unity and not a compound. The discrete nature of this unity has
caused critics to overlook its differentiated character and to
emphasize the figurative, analogical, or referential terms in which
Beatrice appears throughout the *Vita Nuova*: as Christ figure, as
angel, as number nine, as phantasm, as beatifier, as Ciceronian
"friend," etc. ⟨. . .⟩

We must be careful not to pursue any one of the various
analogical or figurative determinations of Beatrice too far, for to do
so leads to insurmountable contradictions. For example, much has
been made of the fact that Beatrice is associated with the number
nine in the *Vita Nuova*, but no one, to my knowledge, has
interrogated Dante's logic in XXIX when he explains that this number
was linked to Beatrice because nine is a "divine" number: the Trinity
times itself. Is Dante telling his reader that Beatrice is or was a
Trinity figure? If so, can she also logically be a Christ figure? And if
she is a Christ figure, can she also logically be an angel figure? And
can she, in addition to these determinations, also be a historical
woman? ⟨. . .⟩

One of the "new" aspects of stilnovism was the hypostasis of love as an abstract and ideal universal. ⟨...⟩

Cavalcanti had declared in "Donna me prega," ⟨that⟩ love has its true place not in the external world but in this imaginary space of memory. But the fact is that the *Vita Nuova* moves both inward and outward, from figure to body, from substance to image, from bedroom to street, and vice versa. The demise of the lord in XXIV in fact marks a decisive turn in the very experience of love, a turn toward exteriority and otherness that commits Dante to the irreducibility of the embodied historical world itself. ⟨...⟩

There is no doubt that the *Vita Nuova* brings the phantasmal dimension of love to a certain extreme with its visions, aesthetic epiphanies, and even hallucinations. On the other hand, if we put the troubadours, the stilnovists, Cavalcanti, and Dante within a single experiential horizon, we are bound to gloss over the way Dante redefines the troubadour and even the Cavalcantian notions of love. Beatrice is both body and image. Dante *does* find himself before her corporeal otherness, and it is precisely that otherness which remains in excess of the phantasm. ⟨...⟩

If Dante resists the closure of Cavalcanti's interiorities; if he places his poems within the framework of an autobiographical narrative, and if much later he embraces the epic alternative, becoming the so-called poet of history, it is because he never ceased to acknowledge the exteriority of Beatrice or the historical otherness of her being in the world. It is this otherness that I have been calling her body.

—Robert Pogue Harrison, *The Body of Beatrice* (Baltimore: Johns Hopkins University Press, 1988): pp. 47, 48–49, 52, 53, 54.

Thematic Analysis of the
Rime Petrose

A kind of furtiveness hovers over much of the critical writing on the *Rime Petrose* ("Stony Rimes"), as though scholars felt a personal embarrassment that the Dante of *dolce stil novo* should have written of sensual, earthy experience as well. Yet the poems' links to both the *Vita Nuova* and all three *cantiche* of the *Commedia* are clear and often profound, and the full development of Dante's poetry and thought cannot finally be charted without allowance for the *Petrose*.

Astrological indications in "Io son venuto" indicate that the *Petrose* probably were composed in 1296 or 1297, after the *Vita Nuova* but before the *Convivio*. The poems' central paradox is that abject suitor and distant lady—the *sine qua non* of Provençal romance—are both present, but that now their sum is anything but courtly. Charles S. Singleton would call the troubadour idealizations "a love without possibility of peace." In the *Rime Petrose*, too, we confront a love without possibility of peace; but here the chivalric rules seem all to be broken as unrequited desire becomes gradually transmuted into ecstasies of violence.

"Io son venuto" follows a strict *canzone* form, each stanza containing two units of three lines each, capped by a seventh to rhyme with the sixth (*abcabcc; defdeff*). Lines 12 and 13 share end-words, as in a sestina, and in all there are five stanzas, followed by a seven-line *congedo*, the last two lines of which also end on a repeated word.

Long before Dante, a poetic tradition contrasted hot human desire with the cold or indifference of nature; the reference to Dido in "Così nel mio parlar" deliberately recalls Virgil's treatment of the theme. In type, then, "Io son venuto" is not altogether new. What is remarkable is both the poems' fastidiousness and its symmetry. Nine lines of each of the first five stanzas follow the trajectory of a different natural process—respectively, the movement of stars and planets; of wind and weather; of birds and animals; of trees and flowers; of rivers and ice. Robert M. Durling has shown that the poems trace a descending spiral, lowering slowly from sky to ground. "Love is only in me and not elsewhere," we are told, and winter is indeed everywhere except in the last four lines of each stanza. These return in parallel to the poet, in whose helpless, hopeless despair each circle comes to rest.

"Io son venuto" introduces the central trope of the *Petrose*: a young girl who is stone-like, both cold to the poet's passion and as rare and beautiful as a precious stone. The one suggestion we have that the poet's life was once different in the past serves only to accentuate the current stillness, which has even annihilated time. The girl's indifference must mean the lover is eternally doomed: "I am certain to bear it ever while I am alive, though I should live forever." Only the *congedo* hints that the season could change, and then this only re-emphasizes that the poet's condition will not. The feeling of paralysis inaugurated in "Io son venuto" ultimately infuses the *Petrose* through to "Così nel mio parlar."

Where "Io son venuto" had acknowledged the *donna petra* as a *donna*, despite her hardness, in the next line of the *Petrose* the comparison is inverted and we are initially presented, not with a lady like a stone, but with a stone like a lady. "Al poco giorno" represents a triumph in the sestina, a form invented by Arnaut Daniel (whom Dante "met" in *Purgatorio* XXVI). Each line in a sestina ends on one of six repeated words, which modulate according to a strict pattern: *abcdef; faebdc; cfdabe; ecbfad; deacfb; bdfeca.* As another shift repeats the first stanza, the poem is then closed by a *congedo*, which uses all six end-words in its three lines.

The only direct continuity between lines occurs at stanza breaks, as the last end-word of each stanza is always the first of the next; only here do adjacent end-words have anything to do with one another. The form thus can seem tortuous, for its elaborate requirements appear more cerebral than poetic. Because the word repetition does become obsessive, however, Dante recognized in the sestina an ideal vehicle for the poetry of unrequited love. The meanings of the end-words deepen with each successive stanza, mirroring the compulsive circularity of sexual longing, hypnotizing both poet and audience. *Ombra*, for instance, at times means "shade," at times means "shadow," and finally connotes the darkness of death; *petra*, which begins as a personification of the lady, culminates in the suggestion of a sepulcher.

"Amor, tu vedi ben," though sometimes described as a "double sestina," is more accurately termed *canzone-sestina* than *sestina doppia.* Marked by a highly symmetrical rhyming pattern, the form demands considerable ingenuity, for only five different words— *donna, tempo, luce, freddo,* and *petra*—are available for ending each of the poem's 66 lines. "Each stanza," notes Donald Sheehan, "begins with one of the poet's verbal obsessions and then, with a full stop at the sixth line, releases him into another one, so progressing until the poet and the poem simultaneously arrive at the end of stanza five where they began: *donna.*" The theme of petrifaction is furthered and deepened, and as in "Io son venuto," water again is turned to ice. We find, as well, the avowals of service and dedication that characterized the troubadours. ("I call out night and day, / only to serve her, for place and time, / nor for any other reason do I wish to live a long time.") Here Dante still endeavors to win the lady, asking his *canzone* to "enter her heart now ⟨. . .⟩ / and drive out the cold." But in the next lines of the *Petrose,* even poetry is defeated as the lover's torment moves beyond the limits of what language can express.

"Così nel mio parlar," the last of the sequence, seems at first glance to break free from the first three *Petrose,* channeling impotent longings into fantasies of violence and revenge. The poet declares at the outset that he means his language to reflect the cruelty of his lady ("So in my speech I would be harsh"), and Dante uses some of the poem's rhymes only here and in the *Inferno.* From the outset, love is imagined as a contest between lover and beloved, each of whom fires arrows at the other—arrows which she can withstand, but he cannot. The threat of the *donna petra* ("I find no shield that she may not shatter") will be echoed by the danger of being turned to stone by the Medusa in *Inferno* IX; and the figure of Love, characterized here as *perverso,* shares that epithet with only one other figure in all of Dante: Satan. As the poem progresses, the lover's praise of the lady's beauty is gradually displaced by obsessive accounts of her cruelty: the poem's language of "gnawing," "chewing," and "teeth" seems to foreshadow the diction of the Ugolino episode, even as its shrieking and paling prefigures Hell itself.

"Così nel mio parlar," as all of the *Petrose,* represents a considerable technical accomplishment, the sensuality and sadism of which may ultimately prove more convincing than the blandishments of the Provençals. Love is again personified, as in the

Vita Nuova, but his function here is solely one of domination or torture. Moreover, though written, like chivalric lyric, to come to the ears of the beloved, this poem declares itself not as a courting song, but as an act of revenge. That revenge, however, is never wholly without desire. The poem ends with a protestation of *vendetta* ("vengeance"), but its more resonant line closes the preceding stanza: "*e poi le renderei con amor pace.*" ("And then I would give her peace with love.") "Così nel mio parlar" couches itself in the language of hysteria and outrage, but finally it, too, is but a shield thrown up by the lover—and duly shattered, in its turn, by the *donna petra.*

For Dante, the *Petrose* may have left their most lasting mark in the ferocity of the language they released. The poems thus constitute not merely an artistic "detour" but a necessary prelude to the *Commedia,* which could hardly have been penned in the dulcet tones of *dolce stil novo.* "Realism," observed Salvatore Quasimodo, "the great poetry of Dante, is born in the '*Petrose*': the emotions are not anagogical but come forth from the flesh whipped by real wind and rain and hail." ❀

Critical Views on the
Rime Petrose

PETER E. BONDANELLA ON DANTE AND PROVENÇAL
LYRIC

[Peter E. Bondanella is Distinguished Professor of
Comparative Literature and Film Studies at Indiana
University. He is the author of *Italian Cinema: From
Neorealism to the Present* (1983) and *Umberto Eco: Signs for
These Times* (1996), and of translations of the *Decameron*
(1982) and *The Prince* (1984). Bondanella here argues that
Dante's stylistic debt to Arnaut Daniel has been greatly
exaggerated: where Arnaut had employed harsh diction, the
Petrose rely more on harsh imagery to achieve a similar
effect of *asprezza*.]

⟨T⟩he many claims put forward for a genetic influence of Arnaut
upon Dante's lyrics cannot be taken as seriously as most critics
believe. There is no doubt that Dante's sestina is modeled
structurally upon Arnaut's "Lo ferm voler," and that his double-
sestina, "Amor, tu vedi ben che questa donna" (LXXIX) is an attempt
to surpass the Provençal master's skill in the sestina form. Apart
from this, the claims for any genetic relationship between Dante and
Arnaut must rest upon similarities in theme, motifs, ideas, and
underlying sentiments about the nature of love which both discuss
in their poetry. ⟨. . .⟩

Both Dante and Arnaut revel in the suffering that sensual desire
causes. Dante's lines—"e io de la mia guerra / non son però tornato
un passo a retro, / né vo' tornar; ché, se'l martirio è dolce, / la morte
de' passare ogni altro dolce" (LXXVII, 62–5)—are similar to several
passages in Arnaut. ⟨. . .⟩

In one poem, Arnaut describes himself as a prostrate lover in
danger of death unless his lady saves him: "per q'eu m'esfortz / de far
e dir / plazers / a mains, per liei / que m'a virat bas d'aut, / don tem
morir / si·ls afans no m'asoma" (IX, 11–7). In another, he pictures
himself as so defenseless against her charms that no shield will
protect him: "de lieis on no·m val escrima" (X, 18). Dante elaborates
this same motif, personifies the force that threatens him as the god

of Love, and gives an even more vivid picture of sexual desire: "E' m'ha percosso in terra, e stammi sopra / con quella spada ond'elli ancise Dido, / Amore, a cui io grido / merzé chiamando, e umilmente il priego; / ed el d'ogni merzé par messo al niego" (LXXX, 35–9). ⟨...⟩

The vindictive element in Dante's most famous *petra* poem, "Così nel mio parlar voglio esser aspro" (LXXX), is similar to lines in which Arnaut consigns his lady to hell if she does not grant his request for the *surplus*: "e si·l maltraich no·m restaura / ab un baisar anz d'annou / mi auci e si enferna" (X, 33–5). The very poem upon which Bowra bases his interpretation of Arnaut's "idealism" contains an exclamation full of the kind of sexual desire that parallels Dante's screams in the *caldo borro* of "Così nel mio parlar voglio esser aspro":

> Hai! si no l'ai, las! tant mal m'a comors!
> Pero l'afans m'es deportz, ris e iois,
> car en pensan sui de lieis lecs e glotz:
> hai Dieus, si ia'n serai estiers gauzire! (XV, 32–5)

⟨In the *Vita Nuova*⟩, sensual love was transcended and sublimated into an agency of man's salvation. Here, the goal in Arnaut's poetry as in the *rime petrose* remains the lady's bedroom. ⟨...⟩

⟨A⟩ more striking aspect of the *petra* sequence is the conspicuous absence of an element important in Arnaut's style—the use of alliteration which Toja calls the most important feature of Arnaut's works. ⟨...⟩ Not found in the *rime petrose*, such techniques abound in the mature style of the *Divina Commedia*. ⟨...⟩

In "Così nel mio parlar voglio esser aspro," the poem which most critics see as the culmination of Dante's harsh style after Arnaut's manner, there is ⟨...⟩ no such alliteration. ⟨...⟩ The *asprezza* of this poem does not derive from either its *hirsuta* (shaggy or rough) vocabulary as Bowra maintains or from its use of *rimas caras* but from the images themselves, such as "Ahi angosciosa e dispietata lima / che sordamente la mia via scemi," "rodermi il cuore a scorza a scorza," "fender per mezzo / lo core a la crudele che 'l mio squatra!," "farei com'orso quando scherza," "scherana micidiale," "caldo borro," and the like, all of which render vividly the stylistic intention to make the speech of the poet as *aspro* as the *bella petra* in her refusal to accept the poet's advances.

—Peter E. Bondanella, "Arnaut Daniel and Dante's *Rime Petrose*: A Re-Examination," *Studies in Philology* 68, no. 4 (October 1971): pp. 418, 422, 423, 424, 427, 428–29.

MARGARET SPANOS ON OBSESSION AND THE SESTINA FORM

[Margaret Spanos has taught at Empire State College of the State University of New York. In this extract, she examines the tensions latent in the sestina form and considers Dante's use of them to deepen the sexual obsession of "Al poco giorno."]

The formal tension between the dynamics of the circular connective logic of the sestina and the labyrinthine logic of the squared form dictating the interlacing rhyme pattern, when raised to a higher degree of abstraction, inevitably suggests the tension associated with squaring the circle. ⟨. . .⟩

The structural tension between the clear onward thrust of the perfect circular form and the labyrinthine complexities of the earthbound squared form is resolved in the final harmony of the mutual and simultaneous completion of both patterns. ⟨. . .⟩ This makes the sestina the perfect emblematic poem which, on all poetic levels, *is* what it means. ⟨. . .⟩

In his sestina *Al poco giorno*, Dante makes his rhyme words—the vehicle of the obsession characterizing the earthbound squared structural dynamic—not only substantives but objects in nature. In addition, he draws his metaphors primarily from the processes of nature. Consequently, he creates a stronger bond than Arnaut between the squared formal pattern and the elemental world. In opposition to both these objects and processes he places his steadfast *desio*, which even as he submits to the processes of time, the winter age, "non cangia il verde." That is, it partakes of the unchanging nature of pure spirit. But the tension of opposites in Dante's sestina is held constant, even intensified, rather than gradually resolved in the experience of the poem. In other words, an achieved synthesis of opposites in the body of the sestina is as logically impossible as Dante recognized the squaring of the circle to be. In the sestina he concludes that a miraculous suspension of the laws of nature would be necessary before such a resolution could take place:

> Ma ben ritorneranno i fiumi a' colli,
> prima che questo legno molle e verde
> s'infiammi, come suol far bella donna,
> di me;   (VI)

However, although the resolution is not achieved on the level of the satisfaction of the poet's *desio*, the *congedo* presents the miraculous principle through which it exists in potential:

> Quandunque i colli fanno più nera ombra,
> sotto un bel verde la giovane donna
> la fa sparer, com'uom petra sott'erba.

Here for the first time in the sestina the lady emerges independent of the poet's desire, asserting her transcendence over the natural objects among which her poetic function had up to now included her. The reader is startled to discover that she has, throughout the poem, embodied in herself the principle of the synthesis. She partakes of the qualities of matter and nature as "la dura petra / che parla e sente come fosse donna" (I), and, simultaneously, of that celestial immutability which makes her immune to natural processes:

> Similemente questa nova donna
> si sta gelata come neve a l'ombra;
>   che non la move, se non come petra,
> il dolce tempo   (II)

Thus her existence is the miracle, analogous to the Incarnation, which makes possible in principle the coincidence of opposites without resolving the particular tension between opposites expressed in the sestina.

The poetics of Dante's sestina may thus be said to stress the stasis of unresolved tension, illuminated by the presence of the miracle which may at any moment resolve it rather than by the gradual progression toward resolution seen in *Lo ferm voler*. This identifies the sense of compulsion in the repositioning within each stanza of the intractable matter of the rhyme words. Thus, while paradoxically holding out the possibility of the miraculous perfection of the circle squared, it strictly limits the experience of circularity to the recurrences of obsession. ⟨. . .⟩

For Dante, and to a lesser extent for Arnaut, the sestina functions as an ideal expression of the impossible union of clearly defined and stable oppositions: the world of nature and the world of spirit; will and obstacle. ⟨...⟩

Arnaut, Dante, and Petrarch discovered in the complex dynamics of the sestina not only an extension of the expressive potential of the poetic voice, but an expanded perception. ⟨...⟩ The form itself becomes, in fact, the basis for a mutual interrogation: by the poet of reality; by the reader of the poet's reality.

—Margaret Spanos, "The Sestina: An Exploration of the Dynamics of Poetic Structure," *Speculum* 53, no. 3 (July 1978): pp. 551, 552–53, 557.

BRUCE COMENS ON THE UNITY OF THE *PETROSE*

[Bruce Comens is a professor of English at Temple University. His books include *Apocalypse and After: Modern Strategy and Postmodern Tactics in Pound, Williams, and Zukofsky* (1995) and *Line of Flight: Fictions* (1998). Here, he reads the *Petrose* against theories of love proposed by Richard of St. Victor, a 12th-century mystic whose writings Dante knew. Comens suggests that the *Petrose* constitute a kind of proseless anti-*Vita Nuova*, narrating a love that descends into hell, much as the *Commedia* later will document a love that leads to heaven.]

"Io son venuto" indicates the narrator's basic situation and briefly predicts his fate; it remains to the other *rime petrose* to explore the various stages on the way to that fate. If we turn now to Richard's *De quatuor gradibus*, we will find it a remarkably accurate guide to those stages. Richard tell us that in the first stage ⟨...⟩ ⟨"⟩the fever of love, often waning but always returning more acutely, gradually weakens the spirit, wears down and exhausts the strength until it completely conquers the soul and lays it low." ⟨...⟩ Each stanza ⟨of "Io son venuto"⟩ shows ⟨the lover⟩ turning from his surroundings back to his love, with the ardor returning more violently each time he does so. ⟨...⟩ Richard calls the first stage the wounding (recall the "crudele spina" [49] of Dante's *canzone*); the second is the binding. ⟨. . .⟩ The irrational obsession that marks the second stage of love is rendered in Dante's "Al poco giorno." ⟨. . .⟩

The vivid simile in the third stanza refers specifically to the lover's bondage,

[⟨. . .⟩ Love who has locked me between small hills
More tightly than cement locks stone.] ⟨78: 18–18⟩

⟨. . .⟩ The third stage of love, according to Richard, occurs when the object of desire becomes unique: ⟨. . .⟩ ["The soul loves one and is devoted to one, it thirsts for and desires the one, it clings to one, sighs for him, is kindled by him, rests in him. In him alone is it re-created and satisfied. ⟨. . .⟩ Who can worthily describe the tyranny of this state?"] This third stage informs Dante's "Amor, tu vedi ben." The claim of singularity would certainly go some way toward accounting for the poem's form, which is unique, as Dante stresses in the *congedo*: ⟨. . .⟩

[Song, . . . I dare to create for this cold object the novelty that is alight through your form, a thing never conceived before at any time.] ⟨79: 61–62⟩

⟨. . .⟩ The lover's situation ⟨in "Così nel mio parlar"⟩, largely an intensification of that presented in the preceding poems, corresponds to Richard's description of the fourth and final stage of love. ⟨. . .⟩ ⟨T⟩he lover turns to revenge in stanza five, beginning with his savage wish: ⟨. . .⟩ ["Would that I could see him split the heart of the cruel woman who cuts mine to pieces!"] ⟨53–4⟩ Again, Richard provides an explanation of this apparently sudden shift to hatred: since nothing, at this stage, can satisfy the lover's desire, the intense love shifts to an intense hate. ⟨. . .⟩ The simultaneity of love and hatred leads to the violent eroticism of the sixth stanza of the *canzone*. ⟨. . .⟩

Even the lover, although unable to save himself, seems to realize something of his fate when he refers to *Amor* not as "Segnor" but as "esto perverso" (41) ["this evil one"], and also when he speaks of his "caldo borro" (60; cf. "burrato" in *Inf.* XII, 10 and XVI, 114). ⟨. . .⟩

In their depiction of a misguided lover's downward path to hell, the *rime petrose* complement the upward movement of the *Commedia*. ⟨. . .⟩ They constitute Dante's first attempt at an objective narrative wherein the speaker is implicitly judged both by what he says and by the manner in which he says it; they are also Dante's first sustained critique of any aspect of love.

—Bruce Comens, "Stages of Love, Steps to Hell: Dante's *Rime Petrose*," *Modern Language Notes* 101, no. 1 (January 1986): pp. 171, 172, 173, 174, 175–76, 182, 184, 186, 187.

SARA STURM-MADDOX ON THE REJECTION OF PIETRA

[Sara Sturm-Maddox is a professor of French and Italian at the University of Massachusetts, Amherst. Her books include *Petrarch's Metamorphoses: Text and Subtext in the Rime Sparse* (1985), *Petrarch's Laurels* (1992), and *Ronsard, Petrarch and the Amours* (1999). In this extract, she examines Beatrice's interrogation of Dante in *Purgatorio* XXX, suggesting that the poet's final rejection of the *pargoletta* of "Io son venuto" constitutes also a disavowal of his earlier and more earthbound views of love.]

Beatrice insists on her own physical beauty ⟨in *Purgatorio* 31:49–54⟩ because it was the physical beauty of another that had replaced her, according to the record of the *petrose*, in Dante's devotion. As if in confirmation, her charge concerning his having abandoned her for another might well take as evidence the emphatic affirmations of an exclusive passion found in the *petrose* poems themselves: "Quand'ella ha in testa una ghirlanda d'erba, / trae de la mente nostra ogn'altra donna," Dante declares of Pietra in "Al poco giorno" (vv. 13–14); "Da li occhi suoi mi ven la dolce lume / che mi fa non caler d'ogn'altra donna," he reaffirms in "Amor, tu vedi ben" (vv. 43–44). In the latter poem, he goes further: ascribing to Pietra's compelling beauty the impossibility of his loving another, he questions whether the beauty of any other woman could compare with that of the unyielding lady of his stony rhymes: he may die of his passionate affliction, he fears,

> per non levarmi se non dopo il tempo,
> quando vedrò se mai fu bella donna
> nel mondo come questa acerba donna. (58–60)

Pietra is antithetical to Beatrice: she is an anti-Beatrice whose destructive power is overcome only by the reassertion of Beatrice's dominant influence. For the experience of the *Vita Nuova* to be definitively reaffirmed, for its continuity with the *Commedia* to be reestablished, the antithetical experience of the *petrose* must be both denounced and rejected. ⟨...⟩

To take the full measure of the reinscription of elements of the *petrose* into the pilgrim's reunion with Beatrice requires a return to an earlier moment of his journey in the *Commedia*, to an earlier evocation of a powerful female figure: to the threatened appearance of Medusa in *Inferno* 9. ⟨...⟩

The primary link between "Io son venuto" and the Medusa episode, ⟨...⟩ lies in the recurrence of rhyme-words from "Io son venuto" in *Inferno* 9, of which the most dramatic is the triple rhyme ALTO-SMALTO-ASSALTO. ⟨...⟩ It is hardly by coincidence that two additional rhyming pairs of "Io son venuto" are found also in *Inferno* 9: SERRA in rhyme with GUERRA, CARCO with ARCO (with the slight variation of the plural: CARCHE / ARCHE). ⟨...⟩

Let us then return to the "pargoletta" of Beatrice's allusion, and to the "petrified" Dante. As we know, the Dante-pilgrim of the *Commedia* did not see Medusa; avoiding the threatened confrontation and aided by angelic intervention, he did "return above," to continue the arduous journey that has brought him at last to the Earthly Paradise. But he *has* suffered petrification, in the experience recounted with passionate force in the *rime petrose*, and the evocation of his petrified state is critical now to the demonstration of his contrition. The contrition of the penitent, attested by his tears, is expressed in a compelling metaphor:

> lo gel che m'era intorno al col ristretto,
> spirto e acqua fessi, e con angoscia
> de la bocca e de li occhi uscì del petto. (30: 97–99)

⟨...⟩ Dante carefully orders the detail of his pilgrim's reunion with Beatrice, not only to evoke the experience of the *rime petrose*, but to dramatize its transcendence. In response to Beatrice's stern rebuke, the thorn that he had proclaimed himself sure to bear eternally is replaced by the sharp sting of the nettle of remorse; in Beatrice's presence, the ice surrounding his heart melts at last; when he at last raises his eyes and looks on her, the violent image of uprooting dramatically renders the wrenching free of a heart that had been "barbato in petra"; and the affirmation of Beatrice's sublime, triumphant beauty definitively cancels the impact, the "colpo," of that fatal beauty that had captivated the poet of the *rime petrose.*

The reevaluation of the pilgrim's earthly experience of love is critical at this point of his itinerary because without it his journey cannot continue. Not only does Beatrice replace Pietra as the fixed sign in the lover's universe; the entire fatalistic and ill-fated cosmos of the *petrose*, that introduced with the astrological determinism of "Io son venuto al punto de la rota," is replaced by a cosmos in which divine grace, not human passions governed by fatal astral influence, determines human destiny.

—Sara Sturm-Maddox, "The *Rime Petrose* and the Purgatorial Palinode," *Studies in Philology* 84, no. 2 (Spring 1987): pp. 125–26, 127–28, 129, 130, 132–33.

RONALD L. MARTINEZ AND ROBERT M. DURLING ON THE *PETROSE* AND THE *COMMEDIA*

[Ronald L. Martinez is an associate professor of French and Italian at the University of Minnesota. He is co-editor of an edition of the *Inferno* (1996). Robert M. Durling is a professor of Italian and English at the University of California at Santa Cruz. In this essay, taken from their 1990 book *Time and the Crystal: Studies in Dante's* Rime Petrose, Martinez and Durling outline some of the structural and thematic elements inaugurated in the *Petrose* and brought to fruition in the *Commedia.*]

An important aspect of the presence of the *petrose* in the *Commedia* is technical: it entails the stylistic and structural gambits associated with the poems. As Russo pointed out, Stazio's treatise on generation in *Purgatorio* 25 is inconceivable without the precedent of the *petrose.* The fashioning of lucid poetry out of dense scientific reasoning—in particular, we note, the language of sexual generation, perception, and the powers of the soul; the use of *rimas caras* (e.g., *-agro, -izzo*); the articulation of Stazio's speech in syntactic periods adding up to canto length (seventy-five lines); the abundance of tropes and figures (*homeoteleuton*, etc.) typical of Dante's most elevated style; a phonic web as densely organized as that of "Così nel mio parlar"—all these features look back to the *petrose*. Nor is this without reason, for the passage, as Martinez has argued elsewhere, is based on the thematics of man as the horizon between corruptible and incorruptible; the production by God of the immortal soul and its joining to Nature's perfected work is itself the horizon, the union of mortal and immortal natures in a substance that is "one in reason." In a fulfillment of the myth of Castor and Pollux, the union with the body of the immortal soul confers on the body its share in immortality. The thematics of man as horizon, fundamental to the *petrose*, appears in the *Commedia* in terms of the Neoplatonic scheme of return to the stars. ⟨. . .⟩

In the *Commedia*, the great majority of astronomical passages describe or include mention of the sun: the "pianeta / che mena dritto altrui per ogne calle" (*Inferno* 1.17–18) functions in the poem as beacon, guide, timepiece, symbol, and chief minister of the heavens through all three *cantiche*. In one sense, its importance culminates in the heaven of Gemini, where it is named "padre di ogni mortal vita" in connection with its role in the nativity of the poet. The importance of the sun in the *Commedia* is similar to its place in the *petrose*, where three of the poems exemplify in their form the principles of the sun's motion and effects: "Io son venuto" imitates the sun's descent to winter solstice; "Al poco giorno," in its spiral movement of rhyme-words, graphs the sun's movement with both Same and Other; and "Amor, tu vedi ben" imitates the changing effects of the sun in conjunction with successive constellations or planets and is arranged axially with *cold* at its center, representing the winter depression of the sun and the central location of a cold earth and the coldness of the lady. Although "Così" appears to lack the sun (see, however, "nel sol quanto nel rozzo," 57), the treatment of the lady's glances as shafts of light anticipates, as we saw, the imagery in the *Paradiso* of the pilgrim's upward motion as a beam of light or arrow seeking its target, and ultimately of emanation and return as the propagation and reflection of light. ⟨. . .⟩

Specific verbal echoes are confirmed by shared thematic concerns and structural principles. The emphasis on the participation of the mind in a cosmic order; mention of divine and human artisanal skill (that of nature is implied); the apparently paradoxical truth that the *departure* of the Other from the Same is required for the wholeness of nature, and thus the idea that the Other—what twists away—must be included in the ambit of Mind, are general notions underlying both the *petrose* and the proem to the heaven of the sun.

—Robert M. Durling and Ronald L. Martinez, *Time and the Crystal: Studies in Dante's* Rime Petrose (Berkeley: University of California Press, 1990): pp. 200, 232–33, 236.

Thematic Analysis of the
Inferno

Dante's Hell is a diorama of sin, enacted as both moral exhortation and poetic prophecy. Change is no longer possible here, and damnation is the irrevocable, total removal from God—a separation that is more terrible for being freely willed by Hell's inhabitants. "What I was living, that I am dead," one soul tells the pilgrim.

Some here are anonymous, bent under the weight of their sin, but the splendor of others is found in their very damnation. Farinata persists in his arrogance; the scorn he entertains is eternal. Yet we cannot but be impressed by him, by Ulysses, by all the towering personalities of Hell—even when their way was wrong. The *Inferno* may not outline our circumstances, but it does outline our condition. Or as James Wood pointedly observed: it is less that Dante's Hell is life-like, than that our life can be Hell-like.

The poem's narration begins on the eve of Good Friday 1300, when the pilgrim Dante awakens in a dark wood, with no memory of how he came to be lost. Repulsed from the hill of Purgatory by three beasts, he appeals to the figure of the poet Virgil, who will guide him through Hell and Purgatory. Beatrice will then show him through Paradise, where Virgil, as "a rebel to His law," may not enter. Three ladies in Heaven prompted Virgil's rescue (**Canto II**). Allegorically, this locates the source of Dante's conversion-journey not in reason or conscience (Virgil), but in divine grace (Mary, Lucy, and Beatrice).

The poets pass the gate of Hell, with its famous inscription, and a vestibule where the neutrals dwell who lived in neither evil nor good (**Canto III**). Here Dante compares the dead souls waiting to cross Acheron to autumn leaves being shed from their branches: sin permits ease of access to Hell. Purgatory has to be climbed; but souls rain into Hell. Dante himself does not pass by way of Charon's boat. Instead there is an earthquake and he loses consciousness, reawakening at the edge of the abyss (**Canto IV**).

According to Dante's poem, Hell is an inverted cone with its base at the earth's center, farthest from God. The first circle houses the unbaptized, spoken for by Virgil himself: "without hope, we live in desire." Dante asks if any have ever left this Limbo and is told of the "Harrowing" that removed Adam and Moses, among others. (The name of Christ, who did the harrowing, never occurs in the *Inferno*; part of the eternal darkness here is the absence of even God's name.)

Minos, at the entrance to the second circle, assigns the damned to their appropriate depth in Hell (**Canto V**). Within, the souls of the lustful are blown about ceaselessly by the winds, as in life they were buffeted unreasoningly by passion. The pilgrim calls on two: the doomed lovers Paolo and Francesca, who had been overcome, she tells us, by that "Love, which absolves no one beloved from loving." We sympathize with Francesca—as does Dante, who faints—yet her account of her trespass should not be taken at face value. Dante may have shown leniency to his sexual sinners, but he did put them in Hell.

As the poets move on, they see rain, snow, and hail descending endlessly on the souls of the gluttonous (**Canto VI**); the avaricious and the prodigal rolling weights back and forth (**Canto VII**); and the wrathful striking at one another in the marsh of Styx. Passing over the river, the pilgrim speaks sharply to "one that weeps," Filippo Argenti, and is congratulated by Virgil for his vehemence (**Canto VIII**). At the city of Dis the Furies threaten them, until an angel arrives to open the gates (**Canto IX**).

Immediately within are an immense number of unbelievers' tombs. From one of these rises Farinata, "lifting up his breast and brow as if he had great scorn of Hell" (**Canto X**). As he and Dante converse, Cavalcante interrupts to ask news of his son. Mistaking Dante's words to mean that Cavalcanti is dead, he cries out in anguish. Farinata continues speaking as if there has been no interruption; we learn from him that the souls in Hell can know the past and future, but not the present.

Lower Hell, Virgil now explains, is partitioned into circles punishing violence, fraud, and treachery (**Canto XI**). Those who dwell outside Dis proper are guilty of crimes of incontinence, rather than of malice, and so are held less culpable than those within. Likewise fraud, a sin "peculiar to man"—and so more offensive because more perverse—is worse than mere violence; and treachery is the worst of all.

Centaurs patrol Phlegethon, the river of blood in which are sunk murderers and tyrants (**Canto XII**). In the dark wood beyond, Virgil instructs the pilgrim to break a branch, and Dante discovers the wails filling the air come not from people hidden among the trees, but from the trees themselves (**Canto XIII**). The souls of suicides, falling here, take root and grow, and Harpies feed on their branches. Or, as Francesco de Sanctis notes: "The hell of the suicides is suicide itself, repeated every moment to eternity."

A rain of fire descends on the souls of the blasphemous, the sodomites, and the usurers (**Canto XIV**). Dante's ambivalence is particularly underscored in the canto of Brunetto Latini, whom he knew to be both immensely admirable as a leader of men—and guilty of sodomy, a sin before God (**Canto XV**).

Virgil now hurls into a canyon the cord with which, in the first canto, Dante tried to subdue the leopard (**Canto XVI**). A creature then rises out of the abyss, his face "the face of a just man" but his body that of a serpent; this is Geryon, the monster of Fraud (**Canto XVII**). He is to carry the poets down the cliff to the ten concentric valleys of Malebolge ("evil pouches").

The first pouch houses panderers and seducers, who are lashed by demons; the second, flatterers who root in human filth (**Canto XVIII**). Simonists are plunged into holes with their calves exposed and the soles of their feet aflame (**Canto XIX**); and diviners, who set themselves against divine will, are grotesquely contorted so they can only see and walk backward (**Canto XX**).

The image of the barrators boiling in tar is typically Dantesque in its vivid evocation of earthly, even mundane, life: "Just so cooks make their scullions plunge the meat down into the cauldrons with their forks that it may not float" (**Canto XXI**). The sinner Ciampolo then tricks the demons, and an all-out scuffle erupts, from which the poets manage to escape (**Canto XXII**).

The hypocrites wear cloaks richly worked on the outside but heavy with lead on the inside (**Canto XXIII**). One among the thieves, Vanni Fucci, is continually burned to ashes and re-formed; still others are tormented by serpents that alter the forms of their bodies, as their crimes have altered the forms of their souls (**Canto XXV**).

The eighth is the pouch of false counselors; Ulysses and Diomed burn here, in a divided flame (**Canto XXVI**). Unlike Homer's,

Dante's Ulysses is not constrained by love of home; instead, he subjected all to his passion for knowledge and experience; his canto itself reads like the "mad flight" it describes. Guido da Montefeltro, in another flame, believed papal absolution could protect him, but at his death his soul was seized for Hell (**Canto XXVII**).

The schismatics of church or state, in the ninth pouch, now are rent in turn: Mahomet has his body ripped open; Bertran de Born carries his own severed head (**Canto XXVIII**). Counterfeiters, impersonators, and perjurers are stricken with a range of diseases (**cantos XXIX–XXX**). And in the circle of the proud, giants are stuck impotently in the ground—among them Nimrod, responsible for the Tower of Babel; and Ephialtes, who challenged Jove (**Canto XXXI**).

The next souls refuse to identify themselves, but willingly give their fellows away, while they are then betrayed in turn—fittingly, in this circle of the treacherous (**cantos XXXII–XXXIII**). Among the most memorable of the *Commedia*'s figures are to be found here, on Hell's floor. Imprisoned by Archbishop Ruggieri, Count Ugolini watched his four sons starve to death; now he gnaws perpetually at his tormentor, clinging to Ruggieri's head like a hood. Other souls are held in the ice with their faces up, so that their tears freeze over their eyes to blind them. We learn that when Fra Albergio murdered his brother and nephew, his soul was taken by Hell even while his body continued to live.

What Dante initially takes to be a windmill turns out to be the giant figure of Satan himself, pinioned forever in the ice (**Canto XXXIV**). Satan, who aspired to the Godhead, is given three immeasurably ugly heads, in a parody of the Trinity, and bats' wings instead of angels'. In his mouths are Judas Iscariot, Brutus, and Cassius, archetypal betrayers of Church and of Empire.

With Dante clasping him by the neck, Virgil descends along Satan's body until they pass through the center of the earth. It is now the morning of Holy Saturday. The poets soon will be able to begin the ascent of the sunlit hill of Purgatory, and they make their first steps toward it by what is now for the first time visible: the light of the stars. ❧

Critical Views on the
Inferno

WILLIAM HAZLITT ON DANTE'S ORIGINALITY

[William Hazlitt (1778–1830) was an influential essayist whose works include *The Characters of Shakespeare's Plays* (1818), *Table Talk* (1822), and *The Spirit of the Age, or Contemporary Portraits* (1825). In an essay on "Sismondi's Literature of the South" in the June 1815 *Edinburgh Review,* he considers how this "severest of all writers" achieved his poetic effects.]

Dante is nothing but power, passion, self-will. In all that relates to the imitative part of poetry, he bears no comparison with many other poets; but there is a gloomy abstraction in his conceptions, which lies like a dead-weight upon the mind; a benumbing stupor from the intensity of the impression; a terrible obscurity like that which oppresses us in dreams; an identity of interest which moulds every object to its own purposes, and clothes all things with the passions and imaginations of the human soul, that make amends for all other deficiencies. Dante is a striking instance of the essential excellences and defects of modern genius. The immediate objects he presents to the mind, are not much in themselves;—they generally want grandeur, beauty, and order; but they become every thing by the force of the character which he impresses on them. His mind lends its own power to the objects which it contemplates, instead of borrowing it from them. He takes advantage even of the nakedness and dreary vacuity of his subject. His imagination peoples the shades of death, and broods over the barren vastnesses of illimitable space. In point of diction and style, he is the severest of all writers, the most opposite to the flowery and glittering—who relies most on his own power, and the sense of power in the reader—who leaves most to the imagination.

Dante's only object is to interest; and he interests only by exciting our sympathy with the emotion by which he is himself possessed. He does not place before us the objects by which that emotion has been excited; but he seizes on the attention, by showing us the effect they produce on his feelings; and his poetry accordingly frequently gives us the thrilling and overwhelming sensation which is caught by gazing on the face of a person who has seen some object of horror. The improbability of the events, the abruptness and monotony in the Inferno, are excessive; but the interest never flags, from the intense earnestness of the author's mind. ⟨. . .⟩ Dante's great power is in combining internal feelings with familiar objects. Thus the gate of Hell, on which that withering inscription is written, seems to be endowed with speech and consciousness, and to utter its dread warning, not without a sense of mortal woes. The beauty to be found in Dante is of the same severe character, or mixed with deep sentiment. The story of Geneura, to which we have just alluded, is of this class. So is the affecting apostrophe, addressed to Dante by one of his countrymen, whom he meets in the other world.

> 'Sweet is the dialect of Arno's vale!
> Though half consumed, I gladly turn to hear.' ⟨. . .⟩

⟨H⟩alf the personages whom he has crowded into the Inferno are his own acquaintance. All this tends to heighten the effect by the bold intermixture of realities, and the appeal, as it were, to the individual knowledge and experience of the reader. There are occasional striking images in Dante—but these are exceptions; and besides, they are striking only from the weight of consequences attached to them. The imagination of the poet retains and associates the objects of nature, not according to their external forms, but their inward qualities or powers; as when Satan is compared to a cormorant. It is not true, then, that Dante's excellence consists in natural description or dramatic invention. His characters are indeed "instinct with life" and sentiment; but it is with the life and sentiment of the poet.

—William Hazlitt, *The Collected Works of William Hazlitt*, A. R. Waller and Arnold Glover, eds. (London: J. M. Dent, 1904): pp. 61–62, 63.

FRANCESCO DE SANCTIS ON UGOLINO

[Francesco de Sanctis (1817–1883) taught at the Zürich Polytechnic and Naples University before serving as

Minister of Education; he has been called the father of modern Italian literary criticism. De Sanctis' major works include *Saggi critici* (1858) and *Storia della letteratura italiana* (1871). This extract, which examines the Ugolino episode (*Inferno* XXXIII), is taken from an article first published in the December 1869 *Nuova Antologia.*]

But how can Count Ugolino, the most eloquent and modern character in the *Divine Comedy*, find a place here, among these petrified beings?

The fact is that Ugolino is here not as a traitor but as betrayed. To be sure, Count Ugolino, too, is a traitor—that is why he is here. But through a most ingenious device, even as Paolo is bound through eternity to Francesca by love, so is Ugolino bound eternally by hatred to Ruggiero who betrayed him. In Ugolino it is not the traitor who speaks but the one betrayed, the man injured in himself and in his children. To his own crime he makes not the slightest allusion; there is simply no question here of his crime. Fastened to the skull of his foe, an instrument of eternal justice, he stands there as a living and impassioned witness to the crime of Bishop Ruggiero. A traitor is there, but it is not Ugolino; it is the head lying under his teeth, motionless, uttering no cry, every expression of life obliterated from it, the most perfect model of petrified humanity. ⟨. . .⟩

The concept of the penalty is the Law of Talion, or the "contrappasso" [retaliation] as Dante would say: Ruggiero becomes the "fiero pasto" [savage repast] of a man he caused to die of starvation together with his children. If the concept were left in these abstract terms, the mode of the punishment would be disgusting and somewhat grotesque; but here the feeling of disgust is immediately transformed into a sublimity of horror, because the executor of the sentence is not an abstract and indifferent instrument of God, but is the victim himself, sating upon his enemy his hunger for hatred and revenge. ⟨. . .⟩

And notice what grandeur of proportions Dante has given to this Ugolino! You would expect to find that this gesture of such extraordinary ferocity would be an adequate expression of his hate, and suffice indeed to strike our imagination with terror; but no! Ugolino is more savage than his deed, he is revealed by that gesture but not appeased by it, like an unsatisfied artist who cannot find his ideal expressed in his work, and despairs of ever achieving it. Ugolino's grief is "desperate," not sated, not placated by that vengeance; his grief is still so alive and powerful that only in thinking of it "pur pensando" [*Hell,* XXXIII, 6], he weeps as if he had just now been hurt. In Shakespeare too we see a father whose children have been murdered. A friend cries to him, "What, man! ne'er pull your hat upon your brows. . . . Let's make us med'cines of our great revenge,/To cure this deadly grief." "He has no children," answers MacDuff. A terrifying answer intimating the hopelessness of vengeance in a father who cannot kill the children of the man who killed his. But Dante's concept is even higher: Ugolino, holding his enemy under his teeth, remains unsatisfied, and not because he desires a fiercer vengeance but because no vengeance can ever assuage his grief or equal his hatred. ⟨. . .⟩

Everything is portrayed larger than life. You do not find yet the true human dimensions, the life-sized statue, but the Pyramid, the Colossus, the gigantic, with which primitive antiquity first gave confused expression to conscious emotion, to the feeling for greatness, for the infinite, which was all the more awe-inspiring as it was less clearly analyzed. This is the secret of these powerful Dantean sketches, so scantily developed, so full of shadows and gaps; by the simplicity of their outline and by effective chiaroscuro, they magnify dimensions and sentiments. ⟨. . .⟩ That wiping of the mouth appalls you, not by the gesture in itself, but because it presents you the whole face of Ugolino with features idealized to befit that gesture; it puts before you the preternatural expression of immense hate, and by that you conceive the infinite.

—Francesco de Sanctis, *De Sanctis on Dante*, Joseph Rossi and Alfred Galpin, eds. (Madison: University of Wisconsin Press, 1957): pp. 110–11, 112–13, 128.

LEO SPITZER ON LANGUAGE IN THE WOOD OF THE SUICIDES

[Leo Spitzer (1887–1960) was Professor of Romance Languages at the Johns Hopkins University and author of

Essays in Historical Semantics (1948), *Essays on English and American Literature* (1962), and *Classical and Christian Ideas of World Harmony* (1963). This extract considers the atmosphere evoked by Dante's extensive use of harsh, Provençal-inspired diction in *Inferno* XIII.]

One distinctive feature of the style of this canto consists in the use, to an extent unparalleled elsewhere in the *Inferno*, of onomatopoeic terms: consider, for example, the following list of harsh-sounding, consonant-ridden words which (often occurring in the rhyme) appear scattered throughout the canto for the purpose of evoking the concepts 'trunk, bush' and 'cripple, mutilate, dismember':

nodosi	fronde sparte	rosta	aspri sterpi	bronchi
tronchi	'nvolti	sterchi con tosco	schiante	scerpi
sterpi	monchi	tronco	scheggia rotta	nocchi
disvelta	stizzo	cespuglio	strazio	triste cesto

⟨. . .⟩ At Dante's hand these become filled with a larger significance; they offer a sort of linguistic, of onomatopoeic rendition of the ideas of torture, schism, estrangement, which dominate the canto (much as the harsh-sounding words served to suggest the ideas of 'crippled' and 'trunk'). Compare, for example, the involved and twisted lines below, which bear in themselves the stamp of self-torture and self-estrangement, and ultimately of infructuous paradoxy:

> L'animo mio, per disdegnoso gusto
> Credendo col morir fuggir disdegno,
> Ingiusto fece me contra me giusto.

After this hopeless entanglement in a verbal thicket, the lines become simple and candid (in the limpid tone of Racine's *Le jour n'est pas plus pur que le fond de mon cœur*), evoking a clearing: one emerges into the bright open sunshine:

> Vi giuro che già mai non ruppi fede
> Al mio signor, che fu d'onor sì degno.

There is here a correspondence between involved sentence and involved feeling, between simple sentence and candid feeling—a shifting of the shape of the sentences according to the shape of mood. In the line *Ingiusto fece me contra me giusto* I hear sounding above the intricacies of préciosité, the note *contra*, symbol of the counter-natural: the repetitions of word-stems (*ingiusto—giusto; me contra me*) suggest the outrage wrought by one half of the human soul against the other; here we may note, to a certain extent, a parallelism with the '*moi dédoublé*' as this is suggested in the most effective line of the second suicide: 'Io fei *giubbetto* A ME delle MIE *case.*' Torture and destruction again form the motif in the lines of Piero that describe the flames of the passion of envy, steadily mounting until all is consumed and honor reduced to strife:

> Infiammò contra me li animi tutti
> E li 'nfiammati infiammar sì Augusto
> Che i lieti onor tornaro in tristi lutti.

Again, in the powerfully charged sentence describing the two-fold activity of the Harpies, we have to do, not only with repetition but with zeugma: *Fanno dolore e al dolor finestra.* The very compression of this line is symbolical of a grief which, although given continual utterance, must endlessly repeat itself nor ever find release. Finally we may consider the pattern, old as epic poetry, '*a* but not *b*,' which occurs three times in as many lines at the beginning of the canto:

> Non frondi verdi, ma di color fosco;
> Non rami schietti, ma nodosi e 'nvolti;
> Non pomi v' eran, ma stecchi con tosco.

D'Ovidio comments on the effect produced by the repetition of the device: he sees therein a deliberate monotony of syntax which "imitates that sort of calm that great stupefaction is wont to produce." But he says nothing about the device itself. To me this negative pattern, with its insistent note of schism, suggests the στέρησις or *privatio* by which, in ancient as in medieval philosophy, the evil is clearly defined as something characterized by the absence of good; Dante would make us see that this forest is a 'wicked' forest.

—Leo Spitzer, "Speech and Language in *Inferno* XIII," *Italica* 19, no. 3 (September 1942): pp. 92, 95–97.

ERICH AUERBACH ON FARINATA, CAVALCANTE, AND CHANGELESSNESS

[Erich Auerbach (1892–1957) was Sterling Professor of Comparative Literature at Yale University. His works include *Mimesis: The Representation of Reality in Western Literature* (1946), *Dante: Poet of the Secular World* (1961) and *Literary Language and Its Public in Late Latin Antiquity and in the Middle Ages* (1965). Below, Auerbach examines Dante's use of "figura" to clothe necessarily static personalities with vividness and significance.]

Imitation of reality is imitation of the sensory experience of life on earth—among the most essential characteristics of which would seem to be its possessing a history, its changing and developing. Whatever degree of freedom the imitating artist may be granted in his work, he cannot be allowed to deprive reality of this characteristic, which is its very essence. But Dante's inhabitants of the three realms lead a "changeless existence." ⟨. . .⟩

Here in Hell Farinata is greater, stronger, and nobler than ever, for never in his life on earth had he had such an opportunity to prove his stout heart; and if his thoughts and desires center unchanged upon Florence and the Ghibellines, upon the successes and failures of his former endeavors, there can be no doubt that this persistence of his earthly being in all its grandeur and hopeless futility is part of the judgment God has pronounced upon him. The same hopeless futility in the continuance of his earthly being is displayed by Cavalcante; it is not likely that in the course of his earthly existence he ever felt his faith in the spirit of man, his love for the sweetness of light and for his son so profoundly, or expressed it so arrestingly, as now, when it is all in vain. ⟨. . .⟩

⟨T⟩he Comedy is based on a figural view of things. In the case of three of its most important characters—Cato of Utica, Virgil, and Beatrice—I have attempted to demonstrate that their appearance in the other world is a fulfillment of their appearance on earth, their earthly appearance a figure of their appearance in the other world. I stressed the fact that a figural schema permits both its poles—the figure and its fulfillment—to retain the characteristics of concrete historical reality, in contradistinction to what obtains with symbolic or allegorical personifications, so that figure and fulfillment—although the one "signifies" the other—have a significance which is not incompatible with their being real. An event taken as a figure preserves its literal and historical meaning. It remains an event, does not become a mere sign. ⟨. . .⟩

⟨T⟩he figural point of view ⟨. . .⟩ enables us to understand that the beyond is eternal and yet phenomenal; that it is changeless and of all time and yet full of history. It also enables us to show in what way this realism in the beyond is distinguished from every type of purely earthly realism. In the beyond man is no longer involved in any earthly action or entanglement, as he must be in an earthly representation of human events. Rather, he is involved in an eternal situation which is the sum and the result of all his actions and which at the same time tells him what were the decisive aspects of his life and his character. Thus his memory is led along a path which, though for the inhabitants of Hell it is dreary and barren, is yet always the right path, the path which reveals what was decisive in the individual's life. In this condition the dead present themselves to the living Dante. The suspense inherent in the yet unrevealed future—an essential element in all earthly concerns and their artistic imitation, especially of a dramatic, serious, and problematic kind—has ceased. In the Comedy only Dante can feel this suspense.

—Erich Auerbach, *Mimesis: The Representation of Reality in Western Literature*, Willard R. Trask, trans. (Princeton, N.J.: Princeton University Press, 1968): pp. 191, 192–93, 195–96, 197.

RENATO POGGIOLI ON FRANCESCA AND LANCELOT

[Renato Poggioli (1907–1963) taught at Harvard University. His works include *Rozanov* (1957), *The Theory of the Avant-Garde* (1962), and *The Oaten Flute: Essays on Pastoral Poetry and the Poetic Ideal* (1975). Here, he foregrounds *quel giorno piu non vi leggemmo avante* ("that day we read in it no farther" [*Inferno* V.138]) and considers what the full story of Paolo and Francesca may imply about literature and illusion.]

At first sight, the final words of Francesca (since these are her final words) seem to be superfluous, and even to lack propriety: they may sound impudent, or at least too complacent, even more than merely unnecessary. What is Francesca's purpose in telling Dante that they did not read in that book any further? Why unveil so deviously, as well as so brutally, those intimate secrets which even a lost woman prefers to keep hidden? Only a harlot, devoid of the last shred not only of modesty, but even of self-respect, would go so far as to speak of her fall in such cynical terms. There is a difference between unchastity and impurity: a woman may be candid without being shameless. In all her behavior Francesca has consistently shown not only great delicacy of feeling, but also tactfulness and good taste. She has given proof of intellectual and moral courage by facing truth in all its nakedness, yet she has constantly avoided the pitfalls of vulgarity and coarseness. If such is the case, we are forced to conclude that her final words must mean something less plain and obvious than what they seem to suggest. I am unwilling to follow the example of some interpreters, who take those words at their face value. The clue we need is perhaps to be found in the very turn of the phrases by which Francesca opens and closes the story of her fall. The first and the last line of that story begin with almost identical words: "one day," "that day" (*un giorno, quel giorno*). In the second case the temporal reference appears to be hardly useful or necessary. It would have been sufficient to say, "and then we read no further." Yet Francesca feels the need to emphasize that they did not read any further "that day." These two small words cannot be explained away as a mere pleonasm, as syllables that are there solely to fill the line. They become pertinent and relevant, and as such, necessary, only if they are supposed to hint or imply that Paolo and Francesca took up again, on other occasions, the reading of the book which had been "the first root" of their sin. Why does Francesca wish to suggest these successive readings, after the one which was interrupted by their first kiss, on the first day of their love? Such a question may not be answered, yet it must be asked. The only thing we need to realize is that Francesca wants us to know that the two lovers returned on other days to the book which once for all has acted as their go-between. The reason for this, as for Francesca's indirect reference to such a fact, may be seen in a wish not so much to recapture the wild happiness of the first, fatal moment, as to recover, if only for an instant, the idealizing and sublimating illusions which literature creates around the realities of sex and lust. It was the worship of passion, the ideology of love, its idolatry and cult, which had hidden from their consciences the danger of damnation and the ugliness of sin; it was the written word, both harmless and harmful, that had spelled their doom. Yet they tasted the intoxicating sweetness of that worship or cult not only before, but even after knowing the bitterness of sin.

—Renato Poggioli, "Tragedy or Romance? A Reading of the Paolo and Francesca Episode in Dante's *Inferno*," *Publications of the Modern Language Association of America* 72, no. 3 (June 1957): pp. 339–40.

KENNETH GROSS ON CRIMES AND PUNISHMENTS

[Kenneth Gross is a professor of English at the University of Rochester. He is the author of *Alice Crimmin's Case* (1975), *Spenserian Poetics: Idolatry, Iconoclasm, and Magic* (1985), and *The Dream of the Moving Statue* (1992). This extract from his essay on "Counterpass" considers the mechanics of Dante's scheme of justice.]

⟨T⟩he pains of the damned are more revelation than retribution; they compose difficult moral emblems which shadow forth sin's inward nature. The Gluttonous, for example, who neglected their souls to pleasure their bodies, their "muddy vesture of decay," wallow eternally in mud—like the pigs which are also emblems of their crime. Tempestuous lovers are whirled forever in a mad, windy storm. Hypocrites walk weighed down by leaden cloaks with ornate gilded surfaces, symbolizing the sinful, false exteriors which burdened their souls in life. Dante's didactic method becomes less objectionable when one realizes that the fallen reader is to be deterred from sin not by threat of retroactive punishment, but by seeing how horrifying his crimes are in themselves, from the perspective of God or the poet. Dante does not predict a future but says, with prophetic literalness, "this is what you are." More generally, we might suggest that the forms of punishment, whatever their pathos, have the ironic structure of satirical images, reflecting Augustine's notion (as explicated by Burke) that sinful "perversity" equals "parody"—the fatal turning of sin yielding a demonic turn or trope on the authentic forms of Christian virtue. For rather than correcting sin, Dante's symbolic ironies show how the infernal states actually perpetuate the spiritual disorder which constitutes sin.

In this sense, we should observe that the moral function and metaphoric structure of the punishments in the Inferno are not strictly commensurable with those of the sufferings meted out in Dante's Purgatory. There, the burdens of the souls eventually blessed are not so much ironic allegories of sin as antithetical, curative conditions: the proud are weighed down with stones, the gluttonous are gaunt and starving, and the envious—the name of whose sin, *invidia*, derives from the Latin for evil or improper looking—have the eyes with which they sinned sewn shut. The Purgatorial states are simpler than those of Hell; they never involve any complex or grotesque reshaping of the human form; and they allow for real spiritual change, as the sufferings of Hell do not. ⟨. . .⟩

That each damned soul knows only the partial truth about his or her moral and symbolic state is a consistent feature of experience in the *Inferno*. But the *conversio* of the pilgrim and the trial of the reader depend largely on the continual effort to bridge the gap between the remarkable things which the self-limited souls say about themselves, and the ironic qualifications or additional knowledge which arise from a more detached view of their words and sufferings. ⟨. . .⟩ In some sense, then, the damned souls are like those condemned prisoners in Kafka's parable, "In the Penal Colony," criminals who are strapped to an intricate ancient machine (the "harrow") which incises into the back of each an exact account of his transgressions, executed in elaborate, hieroglyphic script. ⟨. . .⟩ Likewise, those souls trapped in that machine which is the Inferno have been turned into animated hieroglyphs of sin, pages written on by the hand of God. But in Dante, only the pilgrim and the reader seem to have the potential for real enlightenment; the damned cannot fully decipher themselves, since they have lost true *caritas*, the key to all divine coding. They also lack the free will necessary to pursue fully any restorative act of interpretation. Nor, as in Kafka, will the machinery break down or they die into oblivion, since Hell is eternal and the sinners already dead.

—Kenneth Gross, "Infernal Metamorphoses: An Interpretation of Dante's 'Counterpass,'" *Modern Language Notes* 100, no. 1 (1985): pp. 183, 184–85.

[Teodolinda Barolini is a professor of Italian at Columbia University and author of *Dante's Poets: Textuality and Truth in the Comedy* (1984) and *The Undivine Comedy: Detheologizing Dante* (1992). Here, Barolini highlights the recurrence throughout the *Comedy* of imagery associated with Ulysses, the trespass of whose "mad flight" must necessarily reflect Dante's own.]

The pilgrim flies on the "piume del gran disio," and the saturation of the *Commedia* with flight imagery—Ulyssean flight imagery—is due to the importance of desire as the impulse that governs all questing, all voyaging, all coming to know. ⟨...⟩

The poetic humility of which the later canticles tell cannot simply be taken at face value. ⟨...⟩

Dante is aware of a fact that we tend to forget, namely that he is writing what Bonagiunta says, what Beatrice says, what Cacciaguida says, what St. Peter says. Far from diminishing as the pilgrim draws nearer to his goal, the poet's problems become ever more acute: if the pilgrim learns to be not like Ulysses, the poet is conscious of having to be ever more like him. The *Paradiso*, if it is to exist at all, cannot fail to be transgressive; its poet cannot fail to be a Ulysses, since only a *trapassar del segno* will be able to render the experience of *trasumanar*. ⟨...⟩

The Ulysses theme enters the *Commedia* in its first verse, in the word *cammino,* and more pointedly in its first simile, in which the pilgrim compares himself to one who (unlike Dante's Ulysses) emerges from dangerous waters, "del pelago a la riva" ("from the deep to the shore" [*Inf.* 1.23]) and turns to look at what he has escaped: "si volse a retro a rimirar lo passo / che non lasciò già mai persona viva" ("he turned back to look at the pass that never yet let any go alive" [26–27]). The beginnings of a contrastive Ulyssean lexicon are here established: from "pelago" to "passo," which will be given its Ulyssean twist in canto 2 when Dante asks his guide to ascertain his courage before entrusting him to the "alto passo" (12), thus anticipating the "alto passo" (*Inf.* 26.132) that leads to Ulysses' death. ⟨...⟩

⟨T⟩he pilgrim's concern that "Io non Enëa, io non Paulo sono" (*Inf.* 2.32) is a supreme example of the double bind in which Dante is placed as the guarantor of his own prophetic status: the very act by which the pilgrim demonstrates humility serves the poet as a vehicle for recording his visionary models and for telling us, essentially, that "Io *sì* Enëa, io *sì* Paulo sono." ⟨. . .⟩

⟨T⟩he Ulyssean component of the poem is ultimately related to the *impresa* of the *Commedia* itself, to the poet's transgressing of the boundary between life and death, between God and man. The Ulysses episode is not unique in reflecting Dante's awareness of the dangers of his position: such awareness informs the canto of the false prophets, for instance, which is governed by a need to disavow any connection with what Dante knows he could be considered. The diviners also seek to cross the boundary between divine and human prerogatives; their attempt to read the future in God's "magno volume" (*Par.* 15.50) is an attempt to reach a vantage from which they, like God, "Colui che mai non vide cosa nova," will never see a new thing. And so, these sinners, who would have obliterated by foretelling all the new things before they occurred, whose attitude of conquest toward life's manifold *cose nove* is like Ulysses' toward the "nova terra" (*Inf.* 26.137) he burns to reach, are reduced to being one more instance of the new on the poet's narrative path: "Di nova pena mi conven far versi" (*Inf.* 20.1). But most important from this perspective is Ulysses, most important because the poet makes him so, investing him not only with the unforgettable language of *Inferno* 26 but making his name a hermeneutic lodestone of the *Commedia*, associating it with the voyage metaphor that keeps the Ulyssean thematic alive even in the hero's absence. ⟨. . .⟩ No matter how orthodox his theology (and it is not so orthodox), no matter how fervently Dante believes in and claims the status of true prophet, of directly inspired poet, of *scriba Dei*, the very fiber of the *Commedia* consists of a going beyond. Thus Ulysses dies, over and over again, for Dante's sins.

—Teodolinda Barolini, *The Undivine Comedy: Detheologizing Dante* (Princeton, N.J.: Princeton University Press, 1992): pp. 49, 54, 57, 58.

Thematic Analysis of the
Purgatorio

Orthodoxy set Purgatory, like Hell, underground; Dante, however, conceived of it as a seven-story mountain.

The primal love created Hell for sins—but it created Purgatory for sinfulness. Purgatory's function is not to punish—for the debt of repentant souls is paid by Christ—but rather to cleanse away sinful tendencies. Thus, where Hell endures forever, the *Purgatorio* explicitly adjures us: "think of what follows, think that at worst it cannot go beyond the great Judgement." Souls only pass *through* Purgatory; it is a temporary realm. When the newly arrived penitents are enchanted by Casella's song, Cato scolds them for their delay; this, as the canticle of transition and hope, must be also the canticle of urgency.

Philip H. Wicksteed writes this of the souls on the mountain: "Their torment is itself their solace." The Deadly Sins are purged here, and the pain and suffering are real; yet fundamentally this is a place of mercy, always to err "rather in opening than in keeping locked." Appropriately, Dante made Purgatory serve as the secondary pedestal to Eden, so that the Paradise lost in Adam's sin will be found in our redemption.

After their long descent from Hell, Dante and Virgil pass through the earth to the antipodes of Jerusalem on Easter morning. At the instruction of Cato, Virgil clears the traces of Hell from Dante's face and girds him with a rush. A ship then approaches, crossing the very waters in which Ulysses and his crew drowned, and dispenses a vast number of souls onto the shore (**Canto II**).

Hell's souls are trapped permanently in their own evil; the leaf-like apparitions at Acheron (*Inferno* Canto III), for instance, are driven insensibly forth by divine justice. The will, however, is crucial in Purgatory, which may be why Dante makes Cato its guardian: though a pagan, he is an emblem of the freedom of the will essential to atonement.

The soul of Manfred shows Dante death-wounds on his head and body (**Canto III**). Souls like his, which have delayed repentance or died excommunicated, are required to serve thirty years here in the

Antepurgatory, in compensation for each year lived without grace. Their sentences can, however, be shortened by intercession, and many in this canticle will beg for the prayers of the living. The poets meet Belacqua (**Canto IV**); and Buonconte, who describes how he was saved by a dying appeal to the Virgin (**Canto V**). His account runs antiparallel to that of his father Guido da Montefeltro (*Inferno* Canto XXVII), whose soul, because unrepentant, was confiscated by a demon who sought him for Hell.

Sordello, a Provençal poet, embraces Virgil eagerly as a fellow-Mantuan (**Canto VI**). He then explains to the pilgrim that the mountain can be ascended only by day, sunlight representing the divine guidance without which purgation is impossible (**Canto VII**). The poets are shown a Valley of Princes who had been distracted from spiritual concerns by earthly politics (**Canto VIII**).

Lucy, who interceded for Dante's salvation in *Inferno* Canto II, carries him in his sleep to the door of Purgatory proper (**Canto IX**). Here he ascends three steps, white (contrition), purple (confession), and red (satisfaction by works). A guard traces seven P's on his forehead and unlocks the door with a white (grace) and a yellow (understanding) key, both of which, he explains, must turn for the gate to open.

On the first terrace (**cantos X–XII**), for the purgation of pride, Dante is shown elaborate reliefs depicting examples of humility from religious and political history. The poets then meet a group of souls bent over in penance who are repeating a paraphrase of the Lord's Prayer. (There are few souls on this terrace, because pride is a difficult sin to purge.)

When Virgil tells him to look down, Dante sees on the pavement images of pride, ranging from Satan's fall from heaven to the razing of Troy. An angel then approaches who strikes the pilgrim's forehead with his wing. As they pass along a stairway, Dante asks Virgil why the going seems easier, and Virgil reminds him that with the purgation of each sin the soul's weight is lightened and its progress made less arduous. Dante, reaching his hand to his own forehead, discovers that only six remain of the seven P's marked there.

The second terrace (**cantos XIII–XIV**) opens with voices calling out reminders of envy's antithesis, kindness. Dante sees ahead a number of souls holding one another up; they have their eyes wired shut as penance for their sin.

The poets ascend the next stair, which is less steep, and reach the third terrace (**cantos XV–XVII**), that of wrath. Here, in air clouded with blinding smoke, Dante must particularly rely on the guidance of Virgil (Reason), who admonishes, "See that thou art not cut off from me." The pilgrim walks with Marco Lombardo, who shows him examples of anger from history and myth. As they ascend to the fourth terrace, Virgil explains that pride, envy, and wrath are assigned to the lower terraces, and the less serious sins of the flesh (avarice, gluttony, and lust) to the higher.

The poets now meet penitents who call out examples of "right will and just love," the antithesis of sloth, which is purged on the fourth terrace (**Canto XVIII**). These souls are so eager in their repentance that they can barely remain still even to talk.

A Siren next appears to Dante. Her song distracts men from the pursuit of good (**Canto XIX**). At the rebuke of "a lady holy and alert," Virgil tears the Siren's dress, calling Dante's notice to the stench that is her real nature; and the poets proceed to the fifth terrace, for the purgation of avarice. While they are here, a soul explains that, bound now as they were in life by their stultifying sin, the penitents cannot raise their eyes or move their bodies. When Dante attempts to pay him homage—the soul is that of Pope Adrian V—he is reminded that all here are fellow-subjects of God. After being shown examples of generosity, Dante meets Hugh Capet, who condemns—as a mouthpiece for Dante—his descendants, the royal line of France (**Canto XX**).

A tremor shakes the mountain, accompanied by cries of *Gloria in excelsis Deo*; a spirit has just completed its penance (**Canto XXI**). The spirit, that of the poet Statius, gladly hails Virgil, whose verses helped bring him to repentance (**Canto XXII**). Statius accompanies Dante through the remainder of the *Purgatorio*, even where Virgil can no longer follow.

The poets approach a group whose bodies have been wasted by fasting, the corrective to gluttony (**Canto XXIII**). Dante is then asked if he is the author of *Donne ch'avete intelletto d'amore* ("Ladies that have intelligence of love") (**Canto XXIV**). He delivers his famous characterization of his own art—"I am one who, when love breathes in me, take note, and in that manner which he dictates within go on to set it forth"—and also gives its name to the poetic school of *dolce stil novo* ("sweet new style"). The sixth P then is lifted, and Dante enters the last terrace, that of lust (**Canto XXV**).

Here penitents walk through a fire while calling out examples of sexual virtue (**Canto XXVI**). Dante hesitates to pass through the fire until Virgil reminds him Beatrice will be found on the other side (**Canto XXVII**). When the three emerge, night has fallen again, and Dante dreams of Leah and Rachel. Virgil then explains that he can guide Dante no farther, and that the purgation is complete.

Dante's next steps bring him to Matilda, who explains the nature of the Earthly Paradise she inhabits, and leads him to the pageant of revelation (**cantos XXVIII–XXIX**). Here Dante finds at last the figure of Beatrice (**Canto XXX**). Stricken by awe, he turns to Virgil, but his guide is no longer there, and Dante weeps.

Beatrice scolds Dante for his disloyalty at her death, reproving him for allowing himself to be distracted by the *pargoletta*, or young girl (believed to be either the *donna petra* of the *Rime petrose,* or possibly Lady Philosophy in the *Convivio*) (**Canto XXXI**). Dante faints in remorse, and when he comes to Matilda guides him through the river Lethe, which brings forgetfulness of sin. Her four handmaids then take him back to Beatrice.

Dante, staring at his lady, is temporarily blinded; when his vision returns, the procession has again begun to move (**Canto XXXII**). He then falls into a sleep and wakes to find Beatrice at the base of the tree by which Eve had sinned. Beatrice commands Dante's attention to a series of elaborate allegories to be enacted before them, representing seven disasters to the Church.

It is now noon and the pilgrim is brought to Eden's other river, Eunoë, which restores the memory of right action (**Canto XXXIII**). Taken through it by Matilda, Dante emerges wholly prepared for the journey to be narrated in the *Paradiso,* his ascent to the stars. ❀

Critical Views on the
Purgatorio

PHILIP H. WICKSTEED ON THE INVENTION OF DANTE'S
PURGATORY

[Philip H. Wicksteed (1844–1927) was an influential
economist who also taught literature and philosophy, and
from 1867 to 1897 served as a clergyman in the Unitarian
Church. Wicksteed's works include *An Essay on the Co-
ordination of the Laws of Distribution* (1894), *The Common
Sense of Political Economy* (1910), and *Dante and Aquinas*
(1913). In this extract, he examines the *Commedia*'s
divergences from the Thomist conception of Purgatory.]

Dante regards the mountain of purgatory, then, as the pedestal of
the Garden of Eden, in which Adam and Eve lived their brief life of
innocence,—according to Dante and Aquinas, about six hours. So
when the souls in Dante's purgatory are climbing the mountain they
are literally regaining the very paradise that our first parents lost,
and the second *cantica* of the "Comedy" has a better right to the title
"Paradise Regained" than Milton's poem has. ⟨. . .⟩

⟨T⟩he ordinary conception of the course of human history was
that when man fell, the state of earthly blessedness, being once lost,
became absolutely and eternally unattainable; but through the
grace of God and in virtue of the atoning death of Christ, by faith
and the sacraments, man, though he could not regain the
experience of full earthly blessedness, might pass from the storms
and trials of this life into that higher life, to which Eden was to
have been the prelude. According to this, the Fall permanently cut
out of the programme of man what had been an essential part of
the first conception of the Deity.

Dante apparently could not accept this divine failure, and believed
that if not here, then hereafter, not only must the Heavenly Paradise
be gained, but the Earthly Paradise also must become an actual
experience (and not a mere tradition) for each one of the redeemed;
that so the divine plan for humanity should be realised in its
integrity, and man should know the earth not only as a place of
exile, but as a home, not only as the scene of temptation and trial,

but as the garden of delight, in which he should experience the frank and full fruition of his nature, as God first made it. ⟨...⟩

This ideal naturally affects Dante's whole conception of the nature of the process of purgation itself. This process consists in recovering the lost balance of nature, in erasing the traces of its disturbance, and so in regaining the Earthly Paradise. The mountain pedestal of Eden must be climbed, and its sides are the natural, nay, the inevitable, site of that purgation whose goal is the regaining of its summit.

This is why Virgil is Dante's guide not only in hell, but in purgatory. ⟨...⟩

Virgil, as representing human reason, is Dante's guide to Eden; but he is a guide who knows the nature of the country sought, but does not know the way. Because the only way that fallen men can tread is the way of penitence, opened by the death of Christ, and paved by the sacraments of the Church, which are uncomprehended or unknown to human philosophy. ⟨...⟩

Purgatory with Dante is an opportunity given us of unliving the life that we have lived, and building up for ourselves a past through which "the stream of memory can flow unstained." It gives us the opportunity of living ourselves out of the thing with which we have united ourselves and living ourselves into the thing we have severed ourselves from. So far from being a mere supplement to the sacrament of penitence it is the inner experience and vitally organic process, beyond the grave, to which that sacrament does but admit us. ⟨...⟩

All the forgotten and stray impulses of Eden come back again to him who lives the life of Eden, as the scenes of long-forgotten childhood come back to one who sees again the contour of the mountains or recognises the breath of the flowers amidst which he was a child. It is in the Earthly Paradise that the streams of Lethe and Eunoë flow.

—Philip H. Wicksteed, *Dante and Aquinas: Being the Substance of the Jowett Lectures of 1911* (London: J. M. Dent, 1913): pp. 214, 219–20, 221, 222, 232–33, 238.

[Karl Vossler's (1872–1949) works include *Mediæval
Culture: An Introduction to Dante and His Times* (1929), *The
Spirit of Language in Civilization* (1932), and *Jean Racine*
(1972). In this extract, Vossler details the special
characteristics of Purgatory and its citizens, and considers
the stylistic challenges these must present for Dante.]

A new feeling, a loftier inspiration, a religious fervour growing out
of ethical enthusiasm, transform the fixed frame into a new
structure. If we observe this frame, however, in and by itself, that is,
apart from its poetic enlivenment, it does appear stony. ⟨. . .⟩ If, for
example, not only in Dante's delineation, but in eternal reality, the
serpent of temptation glides every evening into the Ante-Purgatory,
and if it is invariably driven away by two guardian angels, then this
significant vision is transformed into a mere fantasy, and reminds us
of those clocks on German churches or town halls, where at noon
the cock, Death, the twelve apostles, and other puppets go nodding
past us. The speaking trees and voices in the air, the rushes that grow
ever anew, the inevitable earthquake, and similar magical signs of
divine grace lose their vitality, if they are taken literally, and become
mere childish automata. We must not confuse the holy semblance
with the person that bears it nor regard what is emblematic in the
Purgatorio as its poetic essence. ⟨. . .⟩

The human souls in Purgatory have indeed departed this life, but
continue, even after death, their progress and development. They
must make up for what they have neglected, atone for the evil they
have done, but this atonement is under totally changed conditions—
outside of life, without any special activity, and far from their earthly
environment. They must win freedom by wearing fetters, grow
strong by chastening, and perfect themselves by passive endurance.
The figure of the palm tree pressed down with stones, so that it may
struggle aloft more vigorously, would be a good frontispiece for the
Purgatorio. For in the contrast between outward force and inner
impulse lies the peculiarity of the condition of the souls in
Purgatory. In Paradise and in Hell the outward form of the souls is a
likeness of their inner nature. Francesca without her Paolo, Farinata
without his fiery grave, Ugolino without the archbishop's skull—is

unimaginable. In the attitude, the position, the habitation, the environment, of the damned, their inmost character is expressed. They are so vivid as to be tangible.

The souls of Purgatory become intelligible only through their speech. There is something abstract about them; they must explain and express themselves, for they are disfigured by the penalties they endure. In the Ante-Purgatory their bearing is still free and natural; in the true Purgatory it is checked and controlled. So much the more touchingly and vividly does their utterance pour forth. The contrast between their outward and inward condition becomes the mightiest mainspring of the poetry. ⟨. . .⟩ It is their spiritual activity that conditions the visibility of external things. The more completely we penetrate them, the more intelligible does the paradox of their outward semblance become. Their torture, their penance, their disfigurement, reveals itself as something which they themselves have approved, desired, willed, and even created. ⟨. . .⟩ The longer we live with them in their abode, the more completely does the institutional character of this abode vanish.

—Karl Vossler, *Mediæval Culture: An Introduction to Dante and His Times*, William Cranston Lawton, trans. (New York: Harcourt, Brace & Co., 1929): vol. 2, pp. 302, 303–4.

ROBERT HOLLANDER ON CATO AND CHRIST

[Robert Hollander is a professor of European literature at Princeton University. He is the author of *Boccaccio's Two Venuses* (1977), *Studies in Dante* (1980), and *Boccaccio's Dante and the Shaping Force of Satire* (1997). In this extract, Hollander suggests figural associations to justify the presence in Purgatory of Cato, who might otherwise have been consigned to Hell as a pagan, a panderer, a suicide, or a traitor.]

In a way he is a fitting bridge between the two *cantiche*, because he has endured sin, and yet is miraculously saved. The mark of his worldly error is still to be seen in his office, for he must work as

God's customs officer and may not yet complete his purgation and ascend to heaven.

Whatever rationale we may find for his salvation by Dante, we must remember that Dante expected us to be amazed, a fact sometimes forgotten by those who are puzzled by Cato's location. ⟨. . .⟩

Virgil describes the worthiness of Dante to Cato:

> ["Then let it please you to look with favor upon his coming:
>> he goes seeking liberty, which is so dear,
>> as he knows who for it gives up life.
> Thou knowest this, since death for it was not
>> bitter in Utica, where thou didst leave
>> the vestment which on the great day shall be so bright."]
>
> (*Purg.* I, 70-75)

For any Christian the phrase, "he who for liberty gives up life," can point only to Christ's sacrifice. ⟨. . .⟩ The negative presence of Christ in *Inferno* XXXIV—Satan's three heads, perverse figures of the three crosses at the Crucifixion, among a number of other details—has been well noted. And in the following canto Dante again makes us feel the presence of Christ, this time, as is only appropriate, reborn. ⟨. . .⟩

Cato's suicide then, as distinct from the suicidal sin which leads to *Inferno* XIII, is to be thought of, despite the fact that it apparently broke moral and Roman law, as prefiguration of Christ's "suicide." ⟨. . .⟩ The historical Cato's motives are understood by Dante as implying the kind of devotion to liberty that is the mark of Christ, Who sought and found true liberty for all men. And so, for Dante, Cato becomes *figura Christi*. Dante may well think of him as his "father" (line 33). ⟨. . .⟩

That Dante had the canto of the suicides very much in mind when he composed *Purgatorio* I is further evidenced by his use of two words in the two cantos. *Purgatorio* I contains the first of several uses of *libertà* or the adjectives and adverbs formed from it which are to be found in *Purgatorio* and *Paradiso*. In fact, there is only one previous occurrence in *Inferno*, and that is in Canto XIII. Pier has asked that Dante reestablish the memory of him in the world above when he returns. Virgil responds (line 85) by telling him to tell his story to Dante, so that Dante will be able to do freely (*liberamente*) what Pier has requested. Perhaps the cruel point of Virgil's words is that Pier has no liberty at all—he gave that up when he took his own life—while the living Christian he addresses still possesses his freedom. ⟨. . .⟩ The second bit of "verbal figuralism" is even clearer. At the very beginning of Canto XIII Dante describes the boughs of the horrible trees as being "non rami schietti"—branches that are not smooth, but knotted and gnarled (line 5). He uses the adjective *schietto*, smooth, only once more in the poem: *Purgatorio* I, 95. There it describes the *giunco*, which is smooth, and most importantly, the very opposite in its function and its meaning to its Hellish counterparts. The "unsmooth branch" is the "type" of Judas; the "smooth rush" is the "type" of Christ.

—Robert Hollander, *Allegory in Dante's* Commedia (Princeton, N.J.: Princeton University Press, 1969): pp. 123–24, 126, 127–28, 130–31.

RICHARD ABRAMS ON POETS AND GLUTTONS

[Richard Abrams has taught at the University of Texas at Austin. Here, he proposes an explanation for Dante's placement of the stilnovists on the terrace of the gluttonous, rather than with the lustful.]

⟨C⟩onsidering Dante's debt to Guinizelli and the relationship of love poetry to lust, it would have been obvious for Dante to reserve his poetic credo for the next higher terrace in Purgatory, as the circle of lust in *Inferno* offers an introduction to the topic of love literature in the *Comedy*. But the fact remains that, when we wish to review Dante's summary of his objectives as an idealistic young love poet, we are sent back—time and again, irrevocably—to the gluttony cantos. ⟨. . .⟩

In the strategically placed terzina where Gentucca is named, Dante juxtaposes the oral operations of eating and speaking as a shorthand for the antithetical needs of the body and soul. The body must consume, the spirit is prolific. ⟨. . .⟩

By comparing Dante's desire for Beatrice's smile of salutation to Bonagiunta's gluttonous cravings, we enlarge the concept of gluttony to include a related physical dependency, the wish for a love token. The analogy of oral and sexual gratification is a frequent theme in both the gluttony and lust cantos of *Purgatory*, as for example when gluttony is represented as "l'amor del gusto" (XXIV, 152), a sort of food-lust. ⟨. . .⟩

Dante implicitly rejects Bonagiunta's concept of poetic composition which is rooted in the dualism of the act of eating and the process of fertilization-delivery, and replaces it with a metaphor reflecting the monistic, progressive nature of the gluttons' rehabilitation. It is this abrupt shift away from the dualistic framework which the penitents themselves, seeking internal fulfillment, are striving to transcend, that triggers in Bonagiunta a sudden illumination. To appreciate the full impact of Dante's rhetoric, however, it is necessary to distinguish between two concepts of inspiration, one of them dualistic, the other monistic and progressive and thus of a kind with the daily purgative experience of the penitents (or "aspirants" might be the better word).

The insidious metaphor of inspiration which must be ruled out is that which involves the Holy Spirit or angel of temperance replenishing the souls of the gluttons with a breath of knowledge, on analogy with God's breathing of life into the foetus in the womb. What is really going on when we speak of a beatifying inspiration is that the penitents, instead of receiving an external infusion of wisdom, grow wise under stress of their own suffering; their "inspiration" is the revival of their own rational spirits. No longer able to distract themselves through the gratification of invented desires, they turn inward for consolation and so by degrees are initiated into the wisdom of eternal counsel, the Image of God or "Cristo lieto" in their souls. ⟨. . .⟩

Dante's genius as a love poet lies in his decision to design his love-quest as a quest in achievement rather than a quest for favor. ⟨. . .⟩

How Love began leading Dante is narrated in *Vita Nuova*, XIX:

> It happened when walking down a road along which ran a very clear stream, I was so taken with the desire to compose poetry (*dire*) that I began to contemplate the mode I would employ . . . Then my tongue

spoke as though it moved itself, and said "*Donne ch'avete intelletto d'amore.*"

The act of walking and the sight of the flowing stream are catalytic and also emblematic of the way in which Dante's mind is able to toss off a perfect opening line with careless fluency. At this precise moment in Dante's career, the ideal of the pilgrimage through grace is affirmed. Like his inspired tongue, and in contrast to his laboring body, the clear stream "quasi come per se stessa mossa." Like the storm on the heath in *King Lear* that looses Lear's tongue it becomes Dante's inspiration or model, hinting at the possibility of moving in harmony with divine grace, and at the same time giving the lie to the gluttons' dream of remaining in touch with a static source of productivity.

—Richard Abrams, "Inspiration and Gluttony: The Moral Context of Dante's Poetics of the 'Sweet New Style,'" *Modern Language Notes* 91 no. 1 (January 1976): pp. 30, 34, 49, 58–59.

PETER DRONKE ON THE GRYPHON

[Von Peter Dronke is a professor of modern and medieval languages at Cambridge. His works include *Fabula: Explorations into the Uses of Myth in Medieval Platonism* (1974), *Abelard and Heloise in Medieval Testimonies* (1976), and *Intellectuals and Poets in Medieval Europe* (1992). Below, he proposes an alternative to some of the traditional explanations of the pageant in *Purgatorio* XXIX.]

⟨T⟩here is no single instance in Christian tradition of a gryphon associated with Christ before Dante—or rather, before Dante's commentators. ⟨. . .⟩

⟨O⟩n the traditional scholarly view that the gryphon is Christ and the chariot is the Church, the narrative movement would have to be described along these lines. In Canto XXIX Christ descends from heaven to the earthly paradise, in order to pull his chariot, his Church, which (Canto XXX) is crowned by the presence of Beatrice. Then (Canto XXXI) Christ, after performing some optical illusions for Dante and Beatrice, and after being commended for not tearing at the tree of Adam (Canto XXXII), ascends again, leaving his Church behind to be guarded by Beatrice. Beatrice guards it so unsuccessfully that it is annihilated by wild creatures and monsters—so that she at last has to say of the Church (XXXIII 35): "it was, and is no more." ⟨. . .⟩

I have no doubt that, when Dante speaks of the gryphon as "the wild animal that is one person only in two natures" (XXXI 80–1), he is aware of the Christological overtones of his phrase, and is deliberately exploiting them. But that is a very different matter from saying, the gryphon is Christ. ⟨. . .⟩

I would start from my earlier assumption that, as in the visions of Ezekiel and John, inner and outer meanings complement each other, that an outer range of meaning radiates from the inner: here one might say, that the political and theological reverberations of meaning, especially in Cantos XXXII and XXXIII, are rendered possible by a substrate of personal meaning, especially in the three preceding ones. Gryphon and chariot relate fundamentally to the concerns of the protagonists, Dante and Beatrice, and *thereby* to the concerns of mankind.

Thus I would see the symbolically rich meanings of the chariot beginning from a microcosm: the chariot, as in Boethius, the vehicle for a soul—in the first place for Dante's soul, which is crowned by Beatrice. By means of this chariot his soul can travel heavenward and back to earth again. And yet in the nightmarish vision of Canto XXXII Dante sees that wondrous vehicle being degraded and ruined—until Beatrice, who had tried in vain to guard it, and had lamented its ravagings, has to declare it utterly destroyed. Is this not an objective correlative for terrifying inner experiences of Dante's, and must it not relate essentially to the harsh judgment that Beatrice pronounces over him? And when he has been renewed in the stream Eunoe, and is ready to mount to the stars, in the last lines of *Purgatorio*, does the wording not suggest he has acquired a new vehicle of flight for his heavenward ascent—namely, the presence of his beloved?" ⟨. . .⟩

It is only along such lines, I believe, that we can begin to account for the enigmatic range of language used of the gryphon: for the use of divine and Song of Songs language—it is by virtue of what is

divinest in him that Dante is lover of the celestial Bride, Beatrice—
together with expressions and incidents that cannot possibly apply
to Christ himself. ⟨...⟩

Crucial is the passage in Canto XXXI where Beatrice contemplates
the gryphon, and Dante, looking into Beatrice's eyes, sees how, "like
the sun in a mirror . . . the double animal shone in her eyes, now
with certain ways of behaving, now with others (*or con altri, or con
altri reggimenti*). "Reader, imagine how I marvelled when I saw the
thing in itself (*la cosa in sé*) remain changeless, and yet changing in
the image in her eyes"(121–7). Those who identify the gryphon with
Christ must here suppose that in Beatrice's eyes Dante sees the
human and divine natures of Christ alternately. ⟨. . .⟩ ⟨I⟩f we
postulated such a meaning, we would have to admit that the
changeless reality of Christ's two natures in one (*la cosa in sé*) can be
seen by Dante alone, but that with Beatrice's help he can only see it
fitfully—now this way, now that. Beatrice's eyes, that is, would
actually be hindering Dante from seeing "the thing in itself." All that
we know of Dante's thought makes such an interpretation absurd.

—Peter Dronke, "The Procession in Dante's *Purgatorio*," *Deutsches
Dante-Jahrbuch* 53–54 (1978–79): pp. 25–26, 39, 41–42, 43–44.

PETER ARMOUR ON THE SEVEN P'S

[Peter Armour is a professor of Italian at Royal Holloway
College of the University of London, and author of *Dante's
Griffin and the History of the World* (1989). This extract
from his *Door of Purgatory* (1983) argues for several
meanings of the seven P's, further linking them to Dante's
modification of the traditional Purgatory from a place of
punishment into a place of hope.]

The method by which the angel imposes the seven P's suggests the
possibility of multiple meanings in the symbol. Remotely, it recalls
the stigmatization of the saints and the ceremony of Ash Wednesday
already cited with reference to the colour of the angel's robe. More
directly, it rests upon two of Dante's chief visionary sources, the
prophecy of Ezekiel and the Apocalypse (cf. *Purg.* XXIX. 100–5). The

seven P's recall the marking of the Hebrew letter Tau on the brows of the good who are to be saved, and the marking of the foreheads of the elect in opposition to the marks of blasphemy on the seven heads of the Beast and on its followers, before the punishment of the world by the seven plagues of the seven angels. Dante follows these sources in presenting the seven P's also as the signs of the elect (*Purg.* XXI. 22–4). ⟨. . .⟩

All expiation in Purgatory is based upon that performed by Christ (*Purg.* XXIII. 73–5).

The erasing of the seven P's is ⟨. . .⟩ not a remission of the stain of sin, for the souls have already earned this by repentance in life, and Dante knows that he too must die repentant, absolved, and healed of sin (*Par.* XXII. 106–8; XXXI. 88–90; XXXIII. 34–7). ⟨. . .⟩

As the signs of the elements which remain after the *culpa* of the sin has been forgiven, the P's represent primarily the *poenae* or punishments, the reaping of the harvest of sin (cf. *Purg.* XIV. 85). But within this negative context Dante has included the positive idea of the purging-away of those other *reliquiae peccati*, the tendencies to, and habits of, sin. Chiefly by means of the device of the 'whips' inciting to virtue and the 'bridles' for curbing vice, Dante presents his Purgatory as a medicinal curing of the soul, a school of moral training, in the soul's redirection towards virtue and true *caritas*. These examples are nourishments which actually assist in purging away the sin by healing the wound (*Purg.* XXV. 138–9). Their constant presence in the ritual of each cornice helps to decrease the sense of punishment and torment in Dante's Purgatory and gives it a positive dimension of re-education to virtue. ⟨. . .⟩

All these aspects are combined in the word which Dante uses most frequently to describe the seven P's—*Piaga* (wound). This is what the angel calls them (*Purg.* IX. 114), and thus from their first appearance they represent the wounds which remain after sin and which require healing in a process of *ruptio vulneris* and *sanatio mentis*. Dante uses the same word to describe the wound of original sin, healed by Christ becoming man in the Virgin's womb (*Par.* XXXII. 4–6). ⟨. . .⟩

Thus, in three principal senses are the seven P's fundamental to the whole of Purgatory: schematically, as *Peccata*, by their connection with the Seven Deadly Sins; theologically, as *Poenae*, by their importance in the process of progressive remission of the temporal punishment due to sin after death; and morally as *Piaghe*, because their removal denotes the gradual healing of the sinner's soul.

—Peter Armour, *The Door of Purgatory: A Study of Multiple Symbolism in Dante's* Purgatorio (Oxford: Oxford University Press, 1983): pp. 65–66, 70, 72–73, 74, 75.

PETER S. HAWKINS ON OVID AND MATELDA

[Peter S. Hawkins is a professor of literature and religious studies at Boston University, and author of *The Language of Grace: Flannery O'Connor, Walker Percy and Iris Murdoch* (1983) and *Dante's Testaments: Essays on Scriptural Imagination* (1999). In this extract, he shows that by moving from evocations of Ovid to the language of Psalms, the Matelda episode effectively initiates the pilgrim Dante in a new aesthetics.]

She has, of course, been smiling throughout her encounter with the pilgrim; but her smiles contrast with the troubled associations that her amorous appearance has inadvertently inspired him to make. This contrast between who she is and how he has perceived her, between the nature of her Garden and that of the Ovidian bowers he has recalled, is elucidated throughout the rest of the canto as we are led to see the extent to which literature has in fact *not* prepared him for this experience. ⟨. . .⟩

Romance, ⟨. . .⟩ is precisely what is being redefined in *Purgatorio* 28. Having been perceived by the pilgrim as a woman warmed by *amor*'s beams, as a "donna innamorata" (29.1), Matelda chooses now to disclose the truth not only about the Garden, but about her love. From the beginning of his approach, the pilgrim has wanted to understand ("intender," 28.48) what she is singing, to catch the meanings ("intendimenti," v. 60) of her "dolce suono" [sweet sound; v. 59], and in so doing (presumably) to learn how or with whom she is enamored. At last she makes her revelation. Rather than giving her song to him directly, however, she provides him with a biblical gloss:

"Ma luce rende il salmo *Delectasti*, / che puote disnebbiar vostro intelletto" (vv. 80–81). "*Delectasti*" is offered as a satisfaction to the stilnovist suitor who first entreated her, and a "salmo" reveals her song. Citing not the *incipit* of Psalm 91, but the word that opens its fifth (and most familiar) verse, Matelda in effect reorients the pilgrim away from Ovid's poetry. ⟨...⟩

⟨I⟩nsofar as the "*Delectasti*" of Psalm 91 not only encodes Matelda's delight but reaches out beyond the boundaries of Eden, it reveals a way to live joyfully even in a fallen world, provided that one is aware, as the foolish ("vir insipiens," v. 7) and stupid ("stultus," v. 8) are not, how extensively the creation bears witness to the Creator. In the immediate context of the Garden, Matelda's Scripture suggests the perspective of prelapsarian humanity, whereby (as we observe in the "donna soletta" herself) merely to see a field of flowers is to be in love with God and to sing his praises. ⟨...⟩

In *Purgatorio* 28 we see Matelda warm herself with the beams of *this* love. ⟨...⟩

Through what amounts to a "mixed medium" of dance and song and lyric, she makes her creaturely response to the Creator precisely through artistic creation. In so doing, she not only suggests what Adam and Eve might have done before the Fall; she also presents us with the possibility that music and lyric—the work of art—can continue to serve as a form of worship.

If this is indeed the case, then there could be no more fitting gloss to her vocation in the Garden than the text of Psalm 91, epitomized in the single verb she cites, "*Delectasti*." For what we find in the Scripture she alludes to is a raison d'être for the psalmist's own art, a miniature *ars poetica* that underwrites the offering of praise "cum cantico, in cithara"; that underwrites, in fact, the enterprise of Dante's own "poema sacro" [sacred poem; *Par.* 25.1].

—Peter S. Hawkins, "Watching Matelda," in *The Poetry of Allusion: Virgil and Ovid in Dante's Commedia*, Rachel Jacoff and Jeffrey T. Schnapp, eds. (Stanford: Stanford University Press, 1991): pp. 194, 195, 198, 199, 200.

Thematic Analysis of the
Paradiso

Unique in the *Commedia*, the world of the *Paradiso* does not even exist within the poem's story. Instead, it relies—in John Freccero's phrase—on metaphor rather than mimesis. This is the world of symbols rather than real-life sensation.

The poem gives us a picaresque narrative of an ascent through nine heavenly spheres, but the souls Dante encounters in reality *all* dwell in the Empyrean, a realm located beyond space and time. Piccarda, Justinian, Cunizza all appear in their appointed order only as a kind of condescension by Heaven to the pilgrim—and through the *Paradiso* to us. In other words, Heaven is beyond human comprehension, so the inhabitants of Heaven have tried to scale it down to a form the human mind can grasp.

In the *Inferno* and *Purgatorio*, the poet invoked the Muses, sisters of song and daughters of memory; he now appeals not only to them but also to their leader Apollo, since his new task—rendering a peace that must pass understanding—is that much more difficult. Paradise, being wholly divine, can be like nothing human. Dante thus will constantly remind us that the matter he treats is beyond the apprehension of reason or poetry: "In the court of heaven from which I have returned, many gems are found of such worth and beauty that they may not be taken out of the kingdom." Likewise, Cacciaguida's first words are characterized explicitly as being so elevated as to be incomprehensible. Appropriately, given its sublime subject, the poem finds its first prominent image in a myth of violent transformation: the flaying of Marsyas.

Beatrice calls the pilgrim's attention to their progress through space, which he has not noticed. (Their own flight is timed to coincide with Christ's Ascension, which occurred at noon.) The two then enter the moon, whose body envelops them like a cloud, and discuss at some length the theory of the moon spots (**Canto II**). Such abstruse discussions may seem tedious; but if the *Paradiso* is obsessed with doctrine, it is because Dante held understanding to be crucial. As early as *Purgatorio* Canto XV, Virgil compared love to light; and most of the souls are disembodied, lights or gems that vary in size and radiance. We are repeatedly asked to visualize a still greater brightness, and Dante seems obsessed with the sense of sight—because, as Beatrice will note, "[T]he state of blessedness rests on the act of vision, not on that of love, which follows after."

Dante initially takes the real faces in the moon for reflections: like their characters, the bodies of those in this "lowest" of the spheres do not quite realize the fullness of their nature (**Canto III**). The souls in the moon were inconstant in vows; they are ranked not by the type of their beatitude but by a certain deficiency in it. The shade of Piccarda, for instance, was removed from a convent and forced to marry. Her limitation was a limitation of will, which is why she explains that she does not aspire to any higher place because "in His will is our peace."

Beatrice now gives the topography of Paradise (**Canto IV**). When Dante asks if failure in vows can be atoned for through works, she explains that it cannot, for God's greatest gift to humanity is free will, and so there can be no higher act than its voluntary sacrifice— that is, the making of a vow (**Canto V**). Still, there are occasions when the breaking of a vow is a lesser evil than would be its fulfillment.

There now approach a multitude of souls who hail Dante joyously. These dwellers in Mercury do not possess even the faint forms of the moon's faces, but are swathed instead entirely in their own light. The Emperor Justinian, who codified Roman law, delivers an elaborate account of the Roman Empire from its inception through to the rule of Charlemagne (**Canto VI**). And Beatrice outlines to Dante the justice of events surrounding the Crucifixion, reconciling historical contingency with the divine will (**Canto VII**).

Dante enters into Venus so suddenly and swiftly that he only becomes aware of it by the increase of his lady's beauty (**Canto VIII**). This is the sphere of the amorous, and one among them, Charles Martel, addresses Dante. His allusions to the misrule of his grandfather and brother prompts a dialogue on the necessity for human diversity.

Dante next speaks with the lights of Cunizza, who despite her sins of lust succored many of the victims of her brother, the tyrant Ezzelino; and Folco, who condemns corruptions of the Church (**Canto IX**).

Dante and Beatrice now enter the sun, where twelve souls of the wise form a garland around them and dance (**Canto X**). Thomas Aquinas describes the love of St. Francis for a despised woman, the Lady Poverty, whose devotion outstripped even Mary's: "she mounted on the cross with Christ" (**Canto XI**). Aquinas then tells of the founding of the Franciscans, as Bonaventura, a Franciscan, will in turn give an account of the Dominicans. Dante mingles the accounts to emphasize the common mission of the two orders, while reproving their contemporary dissensions (**Canto XII**).

Aquinas further expounds on the perfection of Adam and Christ, comparing the rest of nature to the work of an "artist who has the skill of his art and a hand that trembles" (**Canto XIII**).

After a lecture by Solomon, the light rises, and a new, third circle forms around the first two (**Canto XIV**). Dante finds himself in the sphere of Mars, or the warriors, over which rises the sign of the Cross. Here he meets his own great-great-grandfather, Cacciaguida (**cantos XV–XVII**). The encounter, which is explicitly similar to that of Aeneas and Anchises, seems a reply to the pilgrim's initial protest in *Inferno* Canto II that "I am not Aeneas, I am not Paul."

Cacciaguida greets the pilgrim in Latin, giving an account of a past Florence, and of his own martyrdom in the Second Crusade. Cacciaguida's prophecy resolves the dire predictions made by Farinata and Brunetto Latini in *Inferno* cantos X and IV; but it is also a charge of responsibility for Dante, to his city and to his God.

The pilgrim now ascends into the sphere of Jupiter (**Canto XVIII**). Here the souls spell out *Diligite justitiam qui judicatis terram.* ("Love righteousness, ye that be judges of the earth.") They then form an eagle, the bird of justice.

Dante addressed the problem of virtuous heathen in *Inferno* IV and *Purgatorio* VI, and alludes to it again now (**Canto XIX**). Among the souls in the Eagle are Trajan and Ripheus, who find a place in Paradise despite their pagan origins (**Canto XX**). Dante's conclusion on predestination and divine justice is that, as divine mysteries, they must remain inaccessible to us.

In the sphere of Saturn, the souls of contemplatives descend by a ladder (**Canto XXI**), which Dante and Beatrice will ascend to the realm of the Fixed Stars (**Canto XXII**). In the Church Triumphant,

Gabriel appears as a crown circling the Virgin (**Canto XXIII**). Christ, Mary, and Gabriel then ascend, and Dante undergoes three oral examinations on the theological virtues—by St. Peter, on faith (**Canto XXIV**); St. James, on hope (**Canto XXV**); and St. John, on love (**Canto XXVI**). Temporarily blinded, he passes the third examination sightless before having his vision restored by Beatrice. Dante then speaks to Adam, and the souls all join in the *Gloria Patri* (**Canto XXVII**).

Dante and Beatrice now enter the ninth heaven, the *Primum Mobile*, which sets the motion of all the others. Here Beatrice explains that all nature originates from a point of light, around which the wheels of angels spin in a set hierarchy (**Canto XXVIII**). She also describes how the angels were first made (**Canto XXIX**).

Beatrice's beauty is now such that only God can entirely comprehend it. After his temporary blindness, Dante has his eyes "baptized" in a river of light (**Canto XXX**). He now can discern the Celestial Rose of the Empyrean (perhaps a deliberate contrast with the "funnel" of Hell), in which are seated the ranks of the redeemed.

The pilgrim turns to find that not Beatrice but St. Bernard is to be his final guide in Paradise (**Canto XXXI**). With him now appear Mary, Eve, Rachel, and a number of other Old Testament figures (**Canto XXXII**). The rose is divided to seat those who believed in the Savior before and after his coming; and children are here as well.

Bernard invokes a prayer to the Virgin, asking her to aid Dante (**Canto XXXIII**). The beatific vision that follows is of such splendor the poet frankly acknowledges his failure: "Thus the snow loses its imprint in the sun; thus in the wind on the light leaves the Sybil's oracle was lost." When he next sees three circles, representing the Trinity, Dante compares viewing them to squaring the circle: it cannot be accomplished by reason alone but is granted in a flash of divine grace. The *Paradiso* draws to a close on the same word as had the other two *cantiche*, as the pilgrim finds himself rapt, his "desire and will . . . revolved by the Love that moves the sun and the other stars." ❀

Critical Views on the
Paradiso

JOSEPH ANTHONY MAZZEO ON LIGHT METAPHYSICS

[Joseph Anthony Mazzeo is Professor Emeritus of the Humanities at Columbia University. His works include *Structure and Thought in the* Paradiso (1958), *Reason and the Imagination: Studies in the History of Ideas* (1962), and *Renaissance and Revolution: The Remaking of European Thought* (1965). In this extract, he considers the role and derivation of light symbolism in the *Paradiso*.]

If the problem of the *Paradiso* was the reduction of objects of thought to objects of vision, how was this accomplished? First, the ladder of light constituted an ontological principle which ran through the whole of reality, from the sensible to the intelligible to God. Light metaphysics also unified and made continuous these two orders of reality, by positing light, in its various analogical forms, as the single strand running through the whole universe. To the various forms of light corresponded various forms of apperception, both sense and thought being explained by the union of "inner and outer lights." There was thus no truly sharp cleavage in light metaphysics— at least for the imagination—between the realms of matter and spirit, sense and thought. ⟨...⟩

The gleam of the heavenly bodies is a reflection of God's joy in His creation, as joy in humans is evidenced by light spreading through the pupil of the eye. Recall the passages in *Convivio* III, viii, about sensible beauty as the translation of an inner immaterial quality, an external light reflecting an internal light: Dante is saying here that the sensible beauty and light of the heavens is the "translation" of the immaterial light and beauty which is God. In human beings this translation of the internal into the external light was most manifest in the eyes and the smile. Thus the stars are, metaphorically, the eyes of God: they most reveal His beauty and His joy, they gleam through a kind of rejoicing. ⟨...⟩

The union of the "inner" lights of the faculties of apprehension with the "outer lights" constituting reality releases joy (*delectatio*), in the tradition of light metaphysics—a special application of the general scholastic principle that joy attends the union of a thing with that which befits it (*coniunctio convenientis cum convenienti*). Thus the wisest of men and the great contemplative expound a complementary doctrine. Increase of vision-knowledge results in an increase of love which in turn demands more and higher light. This circular process is characteristic of the ascent from heaven to heaven and ends only when the infinite eternal Light is reached. ⟨. . .⟩

The virtuous triadic circularity of the *Paradiso* describes the way in which consciousness extends its range both *qualitatively* and quantitatively. It describes the progress of consciousness as the development of perception already known and as the successive introduction of new dimensions of insight not derivable from the preceding state. Each moment of Dante's "blindness" as he ascends from sphere to sphere is really the moment of superrational ecstasy which precedes conscious awareness of a new and higher level of reality; this sort of "blindness" comes from an excess of light.

—Joseph Anthony Mazzeo, *Medieval Cultural Tradition in Dante's Comedy* (Ithaca, N.Y.: Cornell University Press, 1960): pp. 104, 106–7, 113, 115.

A. C. CHARITY ON CACCIAGUIDA, EXILE, AND MARTYRDOM

[A. C. Charity was a Fellow of Trinity College, Cambridge, and Lecturer in English at the University of York. He is the author of *Events and Their Afterlife: The Dialectics of Christian Typology in the Bible and Dante* (1966) and *The Waste Land in Different Voices* (1974). In this extract, Charity examines Cacciaguida's prophecy in the context of the entire *Commedia*, interpreting Dante's project as an attempt to explain his life, and his great-grandfather's, as types of Christian martyrdom.]

⟨I⟩t is on Dante that canto XVII chiefly concentrates, and on his 'scendere e 'l salir,' descent and rising, though it is by different steps now than those which the vision as a whole narrates. Of that narrated movement we are, however, first reminded (XVII. 19–23) and then twice more (*vv.* 112–15, 136 f.); but between the first reference and the other two come the clear and deliberate words of Cacciaguida, 'di Fiorenza partir ti convene' ('you will have to depart from Florence') (*v.* 48), and the forecasting of the course of the poet's exile. The juxtaposition of these passages might by itself imply the relation of the narrated story to the story of Dante's life, but in fact the moving passage which stands at the centre of this speech makes the relation plainer still:

> (You will leave everything most dearly loved; this is the shaft that the bow of exile will first pierce you with. You will find how salt another's bread tastes, and how hard the path which goes down and ascends another's stairs. And that which will weigh most heavily on your shoulders will be the vicious and ill company in which you will fall down into this vale.) (XVII. 55–63)

'Scale', 'scendere e 'l salir', 'valle', 'cadrai'—such diction in such a place seems to recapitulate the whole poem in the terms of exile. Perhaps, too, it recapitulates in terms of Christ. For certainly other lines bring Dante's exile into the same kind of relationship with Christ's death as had previously been suggested by the reference to Christ's baptism. The first reference to Christ's death comes immediately before the exile is prophesied ('pria che fosse anciso / l'Agnel di Dio che le peccata tolle', *vv.* 32 f.); then (*vv.* 49–51) we hear that the exile is plotted 'là dove Cristo tutto di si merca' ('where Christ each day is bought and sold'). It is possible, too, that 'ti graverà le spalle' is intended to remind us of the phrase from the gospels already quoted in XIV. 106: 'chi prende sua croce e segue Cristo'. In such a context of allusion the prophecy of Dante's exile has its place; the connotative references are not, as with Florence, of a descent separated from Saviour and Emperor, but of a dying *with* Christ, and it is for this reason possible for Cacciaguida to speak in remarkably joyful terms of his foreknowledge of these sufferings:

> (as comes to the ear an organ's sweet harmony, comes into my sight the time that is being made ready for you.) (*vv.* 43–5) ⟨...⟩

⟨I⟩t is fitting that here Dante should receive the most elaborate and explicit command to declare his vision that he is to have, at the moment when he learns the worst and the best about his future. ⟨...⟩

It is Dante's life which is the literal sense, not the figurative journey into eternity. The figuring, the stylizing, of Dante's life, on this view, remains vital, a necessary means of expressing something he felt about it. It is done for the sake of a point of theology, or, better, for the sake of a claim made by means of typology. But the figuring, as such, has no independent existence: it exists not to replace Dante's personal history, but to interpret it. Without the historical basis, the myth would be meaningless; with it, Dante's claim can be made: this, Dante may say, is my own self-conforming with Christ; Christ's truth has become mine, and I believe that my truth points to his.

—A. C. Charity, *Events and Their Afterlife: The Dialectics of Christian Typology in the Bible and Dante* (Cambridge: Cambridge University Press, 1966): pp. 243–44, 245, 254.

JOHN FRECCERO ON DANTE'S NEOPLATONISM

[John Freccero is a professor of Italian and comparative literature at New York University. He is the author of *Dante: The Poetics of Conversion* (1986), *Dante's Cosmos* (1998), and a translation of the *Inferno* (1994). Here, Freccero explains that, by framing the *Paradiso* as a "command performance" of star-souls, Dante employs neoplatonic means and poetic allegory toward achieving ends that are Christian and theological.]

In the fourth canto of the *Paradiso*, Beatrice enunciates the principle upon which much of the metaphoric structure of the *cantica* depends. She tells the pilgrim that the display of souls distributed throughout the heavenly spheres is a celestial command performance in his honor, a "condescension" of blessed souls from their eternal home in the Empyrean to the upper reaches of sensible reality in order that he might perceive in spatial terms the spiritual gradations of blessedness:

> Così parlar conviensi al vostro ingegno,
> però che solo da sensato apprende
> ciò che fa poscia d'intelletto degno.
> (*Par.* IV, 40–42)

At the same time, it is clear by the inexorable logic of the story (whose principle theme is how the story came to be written) that what applies to the dramatic action applies to the poem itself; that is, heaven's condescension to the pilgrim is matched by the poet's condescension to us. ⟨. . .⟩ ⟨U⟩nlike any other part of the poem, the *Paradiso* at this point can claim no more than a purely *ad hoc* reality. When the pilgrim's ascent to the celestial rose is completed, the blessed return to their seats in the heavenly amphitheater and the heavenly bodies are left to travel in their respective spheres unaccompanied by the family of the elect—no Farinata strikes an attitude here for all eternity. ⟨. . .⟩

Immediately after telling Dante about the descent of the blessed to the planetary spheres, Beatrice says:

> Per questo la Scrittura condescende
> a vostra facultate, e piedi e mano
> attribuisce a Dio, ed altro intende . . .
> (*Par.* IV, 43–45)

We have already noted that the accommodation of heaven to the senses of the pilgrim stands for the accommodation of the poet's experience *per verba* to us, but the pattern for all such accommodation was established by the Bible, the eternal witness of God's accommodation—his Word—to man. Thus, at precisely the point in the *Paradiso* where Dante seems to depart most radically from the Christian tradition, he implies that his accomplishment is essentially an imitation of the Bible. ⟨. . .⟩

Nevertheless, the Christian mystery underlying Dante's representation seems to be clothed in Platonic myth. Beatrice's words in the fourth canto are occasioned by what the pilgrim assumes to be a resemblance of the *Paradiso* to Plato's *Timaeus*, inasmuch as the blessed souls seem to dwell eternally in the stars, "secondo la sentenza di Platone" (v. 24). If Plato's text means what it says, Beatrice denies that the resemblance can be real. If on the other hand,

> . . . sua sentenza è d'altra guisa
> che la voce non suona, . . . esser puote
> con intenzion da non esser derisa.
> (*Par.* IV, 55–57)

The implication is that if Plato intends his account to be read as myth, then it may be taken to bear a resemblance to the representation of the *Paradiso*. Whatever this implied resemblance suggests for the interpretation of Plato, it certainly seems to reinforce the suggestion that the descent of the blessed to the heavenly spheres is in fact a dramatization of the process of myth-making and, as such, is an extended figure for what the poet is himself doing as he writes his poem. The relationship of the true home of the blessed in the Empyrean to the temporary positions they occupy in the celestial spheres is exactly the relationship between Plato's presumed meaning and his mythical account of it in the *Timaeus*.

—John Freccero, "*Paradiso* x: The Dance of the Stars," *Dante Studies with the Annual Report of the Dante Society* 86 (September 1968): pp. 85, 86, 87–88.

GLAUCO CAMBON ON SYNAESTHESIA

[Glauco Cambon has taught at Rutgers University and the University of Connecticut. His works include *Dante's Craft: Studies in Language and Style* (1969), *Eugenie Montale* (1972), and *Michelangelo's Poetry: Fury of Form* (1985). Here, he considers Dante's blending of senses—in particular, sight, sound, and smell—to convey the pilgrim's experience of transcendence.]

⟨A⟩t the very beginning the poet addresses God as the source of light and musical sound; light appears as pure energy, and the heightening of visual and phonic experience combined attains a Dionysian acme ⟨*Par.* I, 75–81⟩ ⟨. . .⟩. Sight and sound ⟨. . .⟩ now manifest the plentitude of Being, and they are conjoined in the act of apprehension. They arouse the poet's desire to know and possess their transcendent source. ⟨. . .⟩ Light, articulate music, motion: again and again these essential attributes of liberated paradisal existence will appear in the most strenuous of the poem's three canticles, to express in the joy of verbal fullness the fullness of a redeemed creation transfigured by direct contact with its ultimate source. ⟨. . .⟩

The keynote was set back in Canto I of the *Inferno*, where mention was made of the Divine Love which first made and moved "those lovely things," and its chordal resolution will ring out at the very end of *Paradiso*, when the climactic vision of Divine plenitude has inwardly attuned the poet's persona to the circular motion imparted by "Amor che move is sole e l'altre stelle" (Love that moves the sun and the other stars). In this pattern a structural counterpoint makes itself heard, if we but remember that what here fills the persona with the blissful wonder of cosmic harmony, conveyed by Dionysian synaesthesia, wailed antiphonally in Hell as the absence of light and music or raged as the combined darkness and sound of fury, likewise expressed by incisive synaesthesia. ⟨. . .⟩

In Dante's vision, the perception of cosmic harmony is a progression of exalting discovery, "ciò ch'io vedeva mi sembrava un riso / de l'universo; per che mia ebbrezza / entrava per l'udire e per lo viso" (*Par.* XVII, 4–6: "what I saw seemed a laughter / of the universe; so that my inebriation / entered through the avenues of hearing and sight"). ⟨. . .⟩ ⟨C⟩ontrolled as it is, Dante's can often become a language of ecstasy and burst the bounds of convention to signify the exuberance of what is inexpressible. Thus, for instance, we get the unison of the just spirits in the composite luminous Eagle of Cantos XVIII–XIX, who fuse their voices and light in an effluence of perfume (XIX, 19–25); and again the short circuit of color, perfume, and word in the choral Rose which is the Church as the community of martyrs:

> (In the yellow of the everlasting rose
> which dilates into grades of splendor and exhales
> a smell of praise to the sun of constant Spring.)
> ⟨XXX 124–26⟩

Blake's dictum that "the road of excess leads to the palace of wisdom" may find a peculiar application here, in the realm where poetry strives to heighten and multiply its powers to match the transcendent experience Dante took as his datum. Synaesthesia pushes his diction to the verge of a trans-language, beyond the logical level, and if it is rhetorically sustained by the strong Dantesque bent for ellipse, it is also fostered by that part of Dante's faith which posited the resurrection of the flesh, thus the eventual glorification of the body and its powers—utter delight being announced to the persona as the final state of the blessed soul (*Par.* XIV, 52–60). In this, the Aristotelian-Thomistic revaluation of the senses as intrinsic to knowledge, against Plato's dismissal of them, helped Dante to find a luminous body for his vision in the very heart of heavenly rarefaction, and recreated for him the possibility of an aesthetic immanence within mystical transcendence.

—Glauco Cambon, "Synaesthesia in the *Divine Comedy*," *Dante Studies with the Annual Report of the Dante Society* 88 (1970): pp. 11–12, 13, 14–15.

MARGUERITE MILLS CHIARENZA ON THE FACES IN THE MOON

[Marguerite Mills Chiarenza is a professor of French, Hispanic, and Italian studies at the University of British Columbia, and the author of *The Divine Comedy: Tracing God's Art* (1989). In this extract, she examines how Dante moves the reader from seeing only images "in a glass darkly," to beginning to conceive of a higher, imageless vision of God.]

In the *Inferno* and the *Purgatorio* the poet's struggle is secondary to the pilgrim's and the danger is essentially in the voyage. In the *Paradiso* it is the poet who struggles while the pilgrim is safe. This is because the pilgrim was in possession of transhuman powers while the poet, who has returned to the human, is not. ⟨. . .⟩ Human categories of perception were left behind with Purgatory. ⟨. . .⟩

In the moon the pilgrim is faced with a vision which seems designed to discourage the senses. The human mind knows incorporeality through spiritual and therefore unsubstantial vision. So incorporeal is the pilgrim's vision that, since his mind is still conditioned to human experience, he falls into the error of thinking it also unsubstantial and turns away looking for what he has taken to be an image. ⟨. . .⟩ But it is not through Beatrice's words, unequivocable as they are, that we first realize the nature of what the pilgrim sees, it is through the image with which Dante describes the pilgrim's error:

> per ch'io dentro all'error contrario corsi
> a quel ch'accese amor tra l'omo e 'l fonte.

The allusion is of course to the myth of Narcissus. ⟨. . .⟩

The encounter with the souls in the moon is clearly an introduction of the concept of intellectual vision. And yet there is one aspect of it which, on the surface at least, seems to go against such an interpretation, encouraging the reader to suppose the pilgrim is not yet ready for a truly incorporeal experience. This is the presence of faces in the description of the souls. In no other part of the *Paradiso* do souls bear any resemblance to the human form. ⟨. . .⟩

Of course, as we have had occasion to say, the poet deals in images and shows us only conceptually what he can have no hope of showing us directly. Still, the form of the human face, in this instance, cannot be understood merely as a necessary imperfection in the representation. It could if there were no emphasis on it, but it is the key image of the passage. Dante compares what he saw, a group of faces, to the reflection of faces in water or glass, and he speaks of a pearl worn on the forehead. The image of Narcissus is the image of a reflected face. Finally, the pilgrim's error consists, dramatically, in his turning his face away from the vision.

Dante's vision could be purely incorporeal but, if it were not direct it would not be intellectual. The whole passage is intended to introduce into the poem the experience of direct spiritual intuition and the image of the face is no exception. It represents the dramatization of the Pauline phrase which was commonplace in describing the directness of intellectual vision, "facie ad faciem," and which was inseparable from its association with the phrase that described all other vision, "per speculum in aenigmate." Everything in the episode works to replace the mirror by the face. In fact, the pilgrim does not yet understand the nature of his vision and consequently puts himself in such a position as to reject it. With the help of Beatrice he corrects his error so that he can then receive the vision granted him. In order to see face to face he must turn face to face. ⟨. . .⟩

Dante could have followed St. Paul and resorted to silence, for of such things "homini non licet loqui" and a poet cannot speak without images. Instead of this he chose to testify to his experience despite the fact that he could only offer an "essemplo," an imperfect rendering and a substitute for the experience itself. From the beginning of the *Paradiso* he confesses that it will be but an "ombra del beato regno," a shadow, a reflection, even an image. Yet from the very first heaven he shows us, through the pilgrims, initial error, that, though we shall see only images, he saw only substances. If he can make us accept this, then perhaps we will accept the climax of his claimed vision, substantial knowledge of God.

—Marguerite Mills Chiarenza, "The Imageless Vision and Dante's *Paradiso*," *Dante Studies with the Annual Report of the Dante Society* 90 (August 1972): pp. 81, 87, 89, 90.

ROBIN KIRKPATRICK ON OBJECTIVITY AND LANGUAGE

[Robin Kirkpatrick is a professor of Italian literature at Cambridge, and author of *Dante's Paradiso and the Limitations of Modern Criticism* (1978), *Dante's Inferno: Difficulty and Dead Poetry* (1987), and *English and Italian Literature from Dante to Shakespeare: A Study of Source, Analogue and Divergence* (1995). Here, Kirkpatrick considers the motives and implications of the uniquely dispassionate diction of the Paradiso.]

⟨W⟩here in the *Purgatorio* speech ⟨*Purg.* VI 76–8⟩ the accumulation of disparate images has a fully expressive force, each phrase making its contribution to the effect of the whole, in the *Paradiso* passage ⟨*Par.* IX 127–31⟩ the 'maladetto fiore' is plainly a figure for the golden florin, inviting one to pause and paraphrase even more obviously than the 'Totila secundus' of 'Eiecta maxima parte. . . ' . The spirit which governs the *Paradiso* passage is a spirit not of expressivity but of analysis. It is, indeed, recognisably the same spirit which in *Inferno* Canto Eleven classified usury as a form of unnaturalness and perverted growth. For within the compass of these five lines, the origin and function of the florin are traced, with a theological eye, to the moment at which the devil turned his back upon the creator of the natural universe. The unnatural flower is no opulently evil 'fleur du mal'. Nor does it possess any imaginative or independent resonance. ⟨...⟩

An even more remarkable, though apparently less important instance, occurs with Dante's reference to Etna at *Paradiso*, Canto Eight, 67–70:

> E la bella Trinacria, che caliga
> tra Pachino e Peloro, sopra 'l golfo
> che riceve da Euro maggior briga,
> non per Tifeo ma per nascente solfo ...

The passage is rich in rhetorical adornment. Yet the final line deliberately eliminates the mythic and imaginative explanation of how the volcano is fired, substituting for this, in its mention of sulphurous vapour, a plainly scientific account. To modern eyes, of course, it is the mythic image that appears the more attractive. However, there is good reason for Dante to suppress its force. For, as Solomon might have taught him, the natural world is as wonderful a subject for contemplation as the world of ancient fable. Indeed, at the very beginning of the Venus sequence, the myths of Venus, by which men once interpreted their relation to the world, are associated with the 'peril' and the 'antico errore' of the pre-Christian era. ⟨...⟩

⟨W⟩hen Carlo speaks, ⟨*Par.* VIII⟩ he appeals neither to fraternal sympathy, nor, rhetorically, to the shame and sensitivity of his audience, nor even to the persuasive logicality of Vergil's 'Né creator né creatura mai. . . '. Rather, throughout the speech he takes wholly for granted the interest and intellectual resourcefulness of his questioner, as one who is independently qualified to understand him. ⟨...⟩

⟨In⟩ one rounded and articulate terzina, drawn with the virtuosity of a Giotto's 'O', he comprehensively formulates the principle upon which his entire manifesto will depend:

> Lo ben che tutto il regno che tu scandi
> volge e contenta, fa esser virtute
> sua provedenza in questi corpi grandi.

The totality of God's goodness, His action as the spur and satisfaction of life, His generosity in the 'delegation' of offices, His benevolence in making possible Dante's own ascent—these are the notions that the terzina brings to order. And to paraphrase in this way is instructive, since, like any other paraphrase, this is a misrepresentation of the original. However in the present case, the misrepresentation arises not from the dispelling of an imaginative effect, but rather from the tendentiousness—which prose so easily admits—of words like 'life,' and images like 'spur' and 'offices'. The strength of Dante's own verse, on the other hand, resides in the pointed and conscious finality with which such phrases as 'fa esser virtute' are produced. Rhythm and syntax here co-operate to impress upon each component a terminological value, so that there can be little doubt that the poet has considered very thoroughly and satisfied himself, at least, about the meaning of such notions as 'making', 'being' and 'virtute'.

—Robin Kirkpatrick, *Dante's* Paradiso *and the Limitations of Modern Criticism: A Study of Style and Poetic Theory* (Cambridge, Mass.: Cambridge University Press, 1978): pp. 98–99, 104, 105.

JEFFREY T. SCHNAPP ON SIGNS OF THE CROSS

[Jeffrey T. Schnapp is a professor of French, Italian and comparative literature at Stanford University. His works include *The Transfiguration of History at the Center of Dante's* Paradise (1986) and *Staging Fascism: 18BL and the Theater of Masses for Masses* (1996). In this extract he argues that, in projecting the cross of light over the sphere of Mars, Dante attempts a reconciliation of historical contingency with eternal grace.]

Superimposed over the cosmos, the cross of light would have appeared a merely abstract figuration of the Christian antidote to the hopelessness of Classical limbo. Rising up instead against the red sky of Mars, it is a brilliantly polemical emblem of hope: a scandalous hope upending all tragic perspectives, infecting with activism all philosophies of skepticism and retreat, promising a true prophetic link between history and eternity, a true genealogical bond between man and his creator. ⟨. . .⟩

Placed within the general setting of cantos 14–18, Dante's cryptic utterance in Greek ⟨14.96⟩ can be easily shown to celebrate the precedence of the cross of Christ over the oracles of Apollo. ⟨. . .⟩ Christ's hermeneutic and epistemological ascendancy over Apollo is, as should by now be clear, one of the central themes in Dante's rewriting of the *Aeneid*'s Book 6 at the center of *Paradise*. The rhetorical fulcrum of Dante's revision is the passage which immediately precedes Cacciaguida's prophecy of suffering and exile:

> (In no dark sayings, such as those in which the foolish folk of old once ensnared themselves, before the Lamb of God who takes away sins was slain, but in clear words and with precise discourse that paternal love replied, hidden and revealed by his own smile. . . .) ⟨17.31–36⟩

Here in capsule form are stated the terms of the supplanting of Classical by Christian prophecy. On the one side stands the madness, the sense of paralysis, the semiotic disorder of the Sibylline (and Anchisean) *ambages*; on the other, the unimpaired clarity of Cacciaguida's prophetic disclosures. Separating them is the sacrifice of Christ, joining them a certain "paternal love" and common "latin" that make of Cacciaguida the Christian double of Anchises. ⟨. . .⟩

Cacciaguida, as the Christian Anchises, does not speak for himself. Rather, he speaks as an intermediary directly transmitting the message of the divine text. ⟨. . .⟩ Descending out of the cross and reascending at the beginning of canto 17, he speaks as the authoritative voice of the cruciform solar Christ—a voice uncontaminated by Mars/*mors* or the flux of history, a voice in which are foreshadowed the distant strains of a universal symphony.

The cross for which he speaks is the same cross prophesied by Virgil, Anchises, and the Sibyls. With its "perpetual insight" (15.65) it promises the translation of Classical tragedy into Christian comedy, Virgil's epic of history into Dante's epic of redemption, the paralyzing riddles of Apollo into the "clear words and precise Latin" of Christian revelation. And in so doing it delimits the powers of human reason and restores the claims of mystery over the province of history. Through this cross Virgil and his prophetic text are completed, but in the process they are superseded and their humanist illusions undercut. This transcendence of Virgil and Apollo is itself encompassed within a broader symbolic act: the inscription of Dante's own poem (whatever its necessary limitations) in God's providential "great volume" through its symbol, the cross of light; and the binding of Dante's own poetic voice through Cacciaguida to the divinely empowered speech of Christ's martyr-prophets. As such, transcribing his ancestor's prophetic utterances, Dante symbolically affiliates his text with eternity itself, over and above all merely human and historical (literary) genealogies. This is the sense in which he touches the limit of his glory and of his paradise ("lo fondo / de la mia gloria e del mio paradiso" [15.35–36]).

—Jeffrey T. Schnapp, *The Transfiguration of History at the Center of Dante's* Paradise (Princeton, N.J.: Princeton University Press, 1986): pp. 86, 139–40, 148, 149.

Works by
Dante Alighieri

Poetry

Rime (including the *Tenzone, Rime Petrose,* and other poems)
Commedia (1314–21):
  Inferno
  Purgatorio
  Paradiso

Prose

De vulgari eloquentia (1307), unfinished
De monarchia (1310)
Epistles (1319)
Eclogues (1320)
Quaestio de aqua et terra (1320)

In Poetry and Prose

Vita nuova (1292)
Convivio (1307), unfinished

Translations of Dante Alighieri's Works

Italian texts:

  Opere. Ed. Pompeo Venturi, 1758.
  Opere minori. Ed. Pietri Fraticelli, 1840.
  Epistole edite ed inedite. Ed. Alessandro Torri, 1842.
  Opere latine. Ed. Giambattista Giuliani, 1882.
  Tutte le opere. Ed. Edward Moore, 1897.
  Opere. Ed. Michele Barbi, 1921.
  Opere. Ed. Giorgio Petrocchi, 1966.
  Opere minori. Ed. Domenico de Robertis and Gianfranco Contini, 1979.

Translations into English:

The Divine Comedy. Trans. Henry Boyd, 1802.

The Vision; or, Hell, Purgatory, and Paradise. Trans. Henry Francis Cary, 1822.

Canzoniere. Trans. Charles Lyell, 1835.

The New Life. Trans. Charles Eliot Norton, 1859.

The Early Italian Poets from Ciullo d'Alcamo to Dante Alighieri. Trans. Dante Gabriel Rossetti, 1861.

The Divine Comedy. Trans. Henry Wadsworth Longfellow, 1867.

The Divine Comedy. Trans. Charles Eliot Norton, 1892.

The New Life. Trans. Dante Gabriel Rossetti, 1899.

Latin Works. Trans. A. G. Ferrers Howell and Philip H. Wicksteed, 1904.

Dante and His Convivio. Trans. William Michael Rossetti, 1910.

The Divine Comedy. Trans. John D. Sinclair, 1939.

The Divine Comedy. Trans. Laurence Binyon, 1947.

The Comedy. Trans. Dorothy L. Sayers and Barbara Reynolds, 1962.

The Odes of Dante. Trans. H. S. Vere-Hodge, 1963.

Dante's Lyric Poetry. Trans. Kenelm Foster and Patrick Boyde, 1967.

The Divine Comedy. Trans. Charles S. Singleton, 1975.

Works about
Dante Alighieri

Anderson, William. *Dante the Maker.* New York: Crossroad, 1980.

Applewhite, James. "The Extended Simile in the *Inferno.*" *Italica* 41 (1964): 294–309.

Auerbach, Erich. *Dante: Poet of the Secular World.* Ralph Manheim, trans. Chicago: University of Chicago Press, 1961.

———. *Scenes from the Drama of European Literature: Six Essays.* Gloucester, England: P. Smith, 1973.

Barbi, Michele. *Life of Dante.* Trans. Paul G. Ruggiers. Berkeley: University of California Press, 1954.

Barolini, Teodolinda. *Dante's Poets: Textuality and Truth in the Comedy.* Princeton, N.J.: Princeton University Press, 1984.

Boyde, Patrick. *Dante's Style in His Lyric Poetry.* Cambridge: Cambridge University Press, 1971.

Caesar, Michael, ed. *Dante: The Critical Heritage, 1314(?)–1870.* London: Routledge, 1989.

Cambon, Glauco. *Dante's Craft: Studies in Language and Style.* Minneapolis: University of Minneapolis Press, 1969.

Clements, Robert J., ed. *American Critical Essays on The Divine Comedy.* New York: New York University Press, 1967.

Colish, Marcia L. *The Mirror of Language: A Study in the Medieval Theory of Knowledge.* New Haven, Conn.: Yale University Press, 1968.

Cook, W. R., and R. B. Herzman. "*Inferno* XXXIII: The Past and the Present in Dante's Imagery of Betrayal." *Italica* 56 (1979): 377–83.

Curtius, Ernst Robert. *European Literature and the Latin Middle Ages.* Trans. Willard R. Trask. Princeton, N.J.: Princeton University Press, 1953.

Davis, Charles Till. *Dante and the Idea of Rome.* London: Oxford University Press, 1957.

De Sanctis, Francesco. *De Sanctis on Dante.* Eds. Joseph Rossi and Alfred Galpin. Madison: University of Wisconsin Press, 1957.

De Sua, William and Gino Rizzo, eds. *A Dante Symposium in Commemoration of the 700th Anniversary of the Poet's Birth (1265–1965)*. Chapel Hill: University of North Carolina Press, 1965.

Dunbar, H. Flanders. *Symbolism in Medieval Thought and Its Consummation in the Divine Comedy*. New York: Russell and Russell, 1961.

Durling, Robert M., and Ronald L. Martinez. *Time and the Crystal: Studies in Dante's Rime Petrose*. Berkeley: University of California Press, 1990.

Foster, Kenelm. *The Two Dantes and Other Studies*. Berkeley: University of California Press, 1977.

Freccero, John, ed. *Dante: A Collection of Critical Essays*. Englewood Cliffs, N.J.: Prentice-Hall, 1965.

Giamatti, A. Bartlett, ed. *Dante in America: The First Two Centuries*. Binghamton, N.Y.: Center for Medieval and Early Renaissance Studies, 1983.

Gilson, Etienne. *Dante the Philosopher*. Trans. David Moore. New York: Sheed and Ward, 1949.

Grandgent, Charles H. *The Ladies of Dante's Lyrics*. Cambridge, Mass.: Harvard University Press, 1917.

Harrison, Robert Pogue. *The Body of Beatrice*. Baltimore: Johns Hopkins University Press, 1988.

Hollander, Robert. *Allegory in Dante's Commedia*. Princeton, N.J.: Princeton University Press, 1969.

Jacoff, Rachel, and Jeffrey T. Schnapp, eds. *The Poetry of Allusion: Virgil and Ovid in Dante's Commedia*. Stanford, Calif.: Stanford University Press, 1991.

Kaske, R. E. "Dante's 'DXV' and 'Veltro.'" *Traditio: Studies in Ancient and Medieval History, Thought and Religion* 17 (1961): 185–254.

Kirkpatrick, Robin. *Dante's Paradiso and the Limitations of Modern Criticism: A Study of Style and Poetic Theory*. Cambridge: Cambridge University Press, 1978.

Kuhns, Oscar. *Dante and the English Poets from Chaucer to Tennyson*. New York: H. Holt, 1904.

Lansing, Richard H. *From Image to Idea: A Study of the Simile in Dante's Commedia*. Ravenna: Longo, 1977.

Limentani, Uberto, ed. *The Mind of Dante*. Cambridge: Cambridge University Press, 1965.

Logan, Terence P. "The Characterization of Ulysses in Homer, Virgil and Dante: A Study in Sources and Analogues." *Dante Studies with the Annual Report of the Dante Society* 82 (1964): 19–46.

Mazzaro, Jerome. *The Figure of Dante: An Essay on the Vita Nuova*. Princeton, N.J.: Princeton University Press, 1981.

Mazzeo, Joseph Anthony. *Structure and Thought in the Paradiso*. Ithaca, N.Y.: Cornell University Press, 1958.

Mazzotta, Giuseppe. *Dante, Poet of the Desert: History and Allegory in the Divine Comedy*. Princeton, N.J.: Princeton University Press, 1979.

Newman, Francis X., ed. *The Meaning of Courtly Love*. Albany: State University of New York Press, 1968.

Reade, W. H. V. *The Moral System of Dante's Inferno*. Oxford: Clarendon Press, 1909.

Rossetti, Dante Gabriel, ed. *The Early Italian Poets from Ciullo D'Alcamo to Dante Alighieri (1100–1200–1300)*. London: Smith, Elder, 1861.

Ruskin, John. *Comments of John Ruskin on the Divina Commedia*. Ed. George P. Huntington. Boston: Houghton, Mifflin, 1903.

Schnapp, Jeffrey T. *The Transfiguration of History at the Center of Dante's Paradise*. Princeton, N.J.: Princeton University Press, 1986.

Scott, J. A. "Religion and the *Vita Nuova*." *Italian Studies* 20 (1965): 17–25.

Singleton, Charles S. *Dante Studies*. 2 vols. Cambridge, Mass.: Harvard University Press, 1954.

———. *An Essay on the Vita Nuova*. Baltimore: Johns Hopkins University Press, 1949.

Thompson, David. "Figure and Allegory in the *Commedia*." *Dante Studies with the Annual Report of the Dante Society* 90 (1972): 1–11.

Toynbee, Paget. *A Dictionary of Proper Names and Notable Matters in the Works of Dante*. Oxford: Oxford University Press, 1898.

Vincent, E. R. "Dante's Choice of Words." *Italian Studies* 10 (1955): 1–18.

Vossler, Karl. *Mediæval Culture: An Introduction to Dante and His Times.* William Cranston Lawton, trans. 2 vols. New York: Harcourt, Brace, 1929.

Wicksteed, Philip H. *Dante and Aquinas.* London: J. M. Dent, 1913.

Williams, Charles. *The Figure of Beatrice: A Study in Dante.* New York: Farrar, Straus, 1980.

Index of
Themes and Ideas

CONVIVIO (THE BANQUET), 12

Dante Alighieri, biography of, 11–13

DE MONARCHIA, 13

DIVINIA COMMEDIA (DIVINE COMEDY), 12, 13, 21, 30, 32, 38, 39–41, 57, 58

ECOLOGUES, 13

INFERNO, 12, 42–58; Beatrice in, 42; Cavalcante in, 43, 52; changelessness in, 52–53; crime and punishment in, 55–56; critical views on, 29, 46–58, 76, 87; De Sanctis on Ugolino episodes in, 47–49; Farinata in, 42, 43, 52; figural point of view in, 52–53; harsh, Provençal-inspired diction in, 50–51; language in, 44, 49–51, 89; language in wood of suicides in, 44, 49–51; Brunetto Latini canto in, 44; love in, 86; Medusa in, 38; originality in, 46–47; Paola and Francesca in, 43, 53–55; Satan in, 45, 46; sun in, 38; thematic analysis of, 42–45; Ugolini episode in, 45, 47–49; Ulyssean flight imagery in, 57–58; Ulysses in, 42, 44–45, 57–58; Virgil in, 42–44

PARADISO, 11, 12, 76–93; Beatrice in, 76, 77, 78, 79, 83, 84, 87–88; blinding of senses conveying pilgrim's transcendence in, 79, 81, 85–87; Cacciaguida, exile, and martyrdom in, 76, 78, 81–83, 92, 93; critical views on, 62, 80–93; dispassionate language in, 89–91; light symbolism in, 76–77, 78, 79, 80–81, 85, 86, 91–93; Love in, 79, 86; moon and imageless vision of God in, 76–77, 87–89; neoplatonism in, 83–85; signs of the cross in, 91–93; thematic analysis of, 76–79; Ulyssean flight imagery in, 57

PURGATURIO, 12, 13, 59–75; Beatrice in, 37–39, 62, 70–71, 72; Cato in, 59, 66–68; character and mood in, 65–66; chariot in, 71; Christ in, 66–68, 70–72, 73; critical views on, 63–75, 76, 87; and divergences from Thomist conception of Purgatory, 63–64; generation in, 39–40; gryphon in, 70–72; language in, 89; Matelda in, 62, 74–75; Ovid and Matelda episode in, 74–75; and *Rime Petrose,* 37–40; *Rime Petrose* and Beatrice's interrogation of Dante in, 37–39; seven P's in, 60, 72–74; stinovists on terrace of gluttonous in, 61–62, 68–70; suicides in, 66–68; thematic analysis of, 59–62; Virgil in, 59–60, 61, 62, 64, 67–68